A QUOTA OF SEAWEED

BY HAMILTON BASSO

NOVELS

The Light Infantry Ball
The View from Pompey's Head
The Greenroom
Sun in Capricorn
Wine of the Country
Days before Lent
Courthouse Square
Cinnamon Seed

BIOGRAPHICAL ESSAYS AND SOCIAL HISTORY

Mainstream

BIOGRAPHY

Beauregard

TRAVEL

A Quota of Seaweed

A QUOTA OF SEAWEED

Persons and Places in Brazil,
Spain, Honduras, Jamaica,
Tahiti, and Samoa

by

HAMILTON BASSO

Drawings by Tom Funk

Garden City, New York
DOUBLEDAY & COMPANY, INC.
1960

For KEITH

All but one of the articles that make up this book appeared in *The New Yorker*, and to one of these, "South Seas Diary," a small amount of new material has been added. The remaining article, "Jamaica Journal," incorporates a number of notes that were printed in *Holiday*, but the larger part of it is now being published for the first time. I am grateful to the editors of *The New Yorker*, and to those of *Holiday*, for permission to reprint.

CONTENTS

Encounter in Puerto Cortés   11

Jamaica Journal   41

The Last Confederate   97

South Seas Diary   133

R.L.S.   181

There Is Indeed but One Ronda   209

CONTENTS

Encounter in Puerto Cortés

ENCOUNTER IN PUERTO CORTÉS

SEVEN years ago, in midsummer, I sailed aboard a Norwegian freighter that was making a two-week run from New York to Rio. I was one of ten passengers, and we were rather a mixed lot. The others were an extremely attractive blond girl, who turned out to be the youngest princess of one of the royal Scandinavian houses and who could not have more charmingly underplayed her hand; her wealthy commoner husband of a few months' standing, who was somewhat less relaxed; an energetic Brazilian who had been born deep in the head-hunter country of the Amazon, where his father had some sort of government job, and who now owned an import-export business in New York and lived in Brooklyn; his wife, an ample lady of Pennsylvania-Dutch extraction, who had a surprising passion for sun suits; a young French-Canadian schoolteacher on her way to a new post, in a convent school in São Paulo; the platinum-blond California-born wife of a coffee broker in Santos, who spent a large part of the voyage in curlers; a shy Argentine girl returning home after a year spent as an exchange student in the United States; a displaced Pole who had hopes of making a go of it in Brazil; and, finally, a short, square woman of advanced middle age, whose appearance was so undistinguished that I find it hard to say what she looked like.

A loose pile of hair, a pair of steel-rimmed spectacles, and a nondescript costume in which she seemed more swaddled than dressed—that's all I remember, and not so clearly that I'd want to gamble on it. I can't recall the color of the eyes behind the spectacles, nor do I know if I'm right in thinking that she had a faint mustache, and, for the life of me, I wouldn't be able to swear to what that day-in-day-out costume of hers consisted of—a gray wool skirt, maybe, maybe a brownish sweater, and maybe gray wool stockings and a pair of heavy walking shoes. I just don't know.

I wasn't quite as friendly to this lady as I might have been—a breach of shipboard manners that I'm not exactly proud of. But word gets around quickly on a freighter, and the word about her was that she might best be avoided. It was the chief engineer who tipped me off. She sat at his table. He told me that she was the Ancient Mariner type, only more so: let her get her conversational hooks into me and it wouldn't be merely for the duration of a wedding feast, it would be for all those days at sea. The chief was a kind man, in his late forties—one of the dark-haired Norwegians and beginning to go bald. He signed on for his first berth when he was sixteen, and in the course of the next thirty-two years he had been just about every-where. Once I commented on his knowledge of the earth's surface. He gave a shrug—"A man goes here, he goes there, and he picks up his quota of seaweed."

14

Though the chief liked the New York–Rio run, away from the storms and the cold of the North Atlantic, he missed his wife and children, who were in Stavanger. He hadn't been there in nearly three years. He kept up a running letter to his wife, adding something every day, and he was proud of a cactus garden in his cabin, grown in a large array of pots—he must have had twenty different varieties, some of which were in bloom. It was unlike him to speak harshly of anyone, but the lady in question had apparently lost no time in getting on his nerves. Her name, I'll say, was Mrs. Schenck, and she was traveling on a Netherlands passport. She would try to corner the chief after meals, and he took to getting up abruptly from dinner and disappearing into his cabin. I'd join him there for coffee and then a drink or two, and invariably he would start talking about Mrs. Schenck, just as a way of getting rid of his irritation.

By the time we reached flying-fish waters, the chief had managed to convince himself that Mrs. Schenck was slightly mad. Who but a madwoman, he asked me, would have no home anywhere—not even a room in a boarding-house? Who but a madwoman would go traveling about the world year after year, never coming to rest? She made him uncomfortable. There was something wrong with her. And the way she talked—on, on, and on. Take his advice and give her a wide berth.

As it happened, this wasn't difficult for me to do. It was Mrs. Schenck's habit to buttonhole her victims at meal-time, and I was seated at another table, with my back to her. Still, I was close enough to hear her talking, and now and then—even though she habitually spoke a thick, guttural, heavily accented English that wasn't easy to understand—I found myself listening to her accounts of her travels. One story would be about the Belgian Congo, another about a village in Japan, another about a train ride in Anatolia. You got the impression that she kept forever on the move—that if she spent as much as two days in one place it was a long stay.

I began to think of her as the Compulsive Traveler. A couple of stories she told stuck in my mind. One had to do with the time she happened to hear something about the airport at Gander, Newfoundland, and decided she wanted to go there; she boarded a plane in Paris, flew to Gander, had a look at the airport, and took the next plane back to Europe. And another time, in the summer of 1939, just before the outbreak of the Second World War, she went to Poland with the sole idea of visiting the salt mines near Kraków. That done, she moved on to Latvia.

One's first impulse was to suspect not only that Mrs. Schenck had a talent for tall tales but that some kind of psychopathic imagination was at work in her. What prevented one from being sure was the fact that some of the rest of us were acquainted with a good many of the places she said she had been to, and that she was never caught in even the smallest error. Our displaced Pole had been born near Kraków, our first mate knew parts of the Belgian Congo very well, our platinum blonde had twice come down at Gander, and our radio operator was familiar with

Japan. Mrs. Schenck never mentioned a detail that didn't jibe with their firsthand knowledge.

Slightly mad she might be, then, but she was not a fake. That was our verdict. And the explanation she gave for her ceaseless voyaging was perfectly plausible; her husband had been a moderately wealthy millowner, she said, and after his death she had made up her mind to see the world—all the old places she had read about as a girl, and all the new places, like Gander, that she had heard about more recently. She had no children, no relatives, no ties. Travel was solace, family, and friend.

Nearly all this I got from the chief, sitting in his cabin among his cactus plants and photographs of his wife and children. I doubt whether Mrs. Schenck and I exchanged ten words during that whole two-week voyage; I know I saw her on deck only once. She was bent over a long stringy piece of knitting, which she was hardly ever without, even in the dining room. Her lips were moving, as if she were counting stitches, and she lifted her head in a quick, jerky motion—an impatient motion, I thought—as my shadow fell across her work. I never did get a really good look at her.

After I reached Brazil, I caught myself thinking about Mrs. Schenck once or twice—truly a curious woman—and late one evening in Rio, as I was leaving my hotel, I thought I saw her sitting in an overcrowded trolley. I was anything but sure, however. It could have been Mrs. Schenck and it could have been anybody. What faint impression I had of her was already beginning to fade. Eventually I returned to the United States, where it faded completely, and it was not until fairly recently, when I was in the banana port of Puerto Cortés, Honduras, that I had cause to think of her again.

Lest it be thought that I am something of a compulsive traveler myself, I should explain that I went to Puerto Cortés on a specific mission, meaning to use it as a jumping-off place for the ruins of an ancient Indian city near Copán, up in the Honduran hills. That, though, is another story. It is enough right now to say that I had voyaged to Puerto Cortés from New York on a banana boat; that at about one o'clock on the afternoon of our arrival we were waiting at anchor in the harbor while one of our sister ships finished taking on bananas at the only dock; and that it was blazing, blazing hot. There is almost always some kind of breeze on the water—some faint breath, at least—but not that day. The waters of the harbor looked thick and nearly solid, like half-molten glass. The decks were hot as skillets. A pair of big black buzzards floated over the town, which was stretched out along one side of a semicircular bay, and you could see the heat shimmering from the tin roofs of the houses cluttered beyond the wharf. The hills behind the town were a still, heavy, intense green. The sky seemed never to have known a cloud. As I looked up at it, watching the buzzards, my eyes ached.

Some of our crew had permission to go ashore, and a beat-up launch came to ferry them to Puerto Cortés, along with anybody else who wanted to go. Despite the heat, I wanted to. I had a few letters to mail, and, besides, I was interested in Puerto Cortés. My proposed trip to Copán had already been canceled by wireless because of a tangle of complications that I needn't go into, and Puerto Cortés was all I had to fall back on. I didn't feel too put upon, however. I had never been in a Central American banana port before, and this was my first visit to Honduras.

When I was first told that my boat would put in at Puerto Cortés, I had begun reading up on the place, and I had developed a certain amount of curiosity about it. As its name suggests, it ties in with Cortés' plundering of the New World. By 1524—twenty-two years after Columbus, on his fourth voyage, first set foot on the American mainland, at a point about a hundred miles down the coast from Puerto Cortés—the conquistador had pillaged Mexico more or less clean and, hearing of more cities to be looted farther south, dispatched one of his commanders, Cristóbal de Olid, to establish a beachhead in Honduras.

Around the time Olid set forth, another Spanish adventurer, Gil González Dávila, who was sailing from Santo Domingo to Nicaragua, steered too far to the west and fetched up off the Honduran coast, about where Puerto Cortés is now. A bad storm arose before he could land, and in order to lighten his ship he was forced to throw some of his horses overboard. He named the place Puerto Caballos, to memorialize the incident, and went on his way. When Olid arrived some weeks later, he pitched camp about eight miles to the southwest, near what is now the coastal town of Omoa, and, fired by ambitions that

had apparently got the better of him during his voyage,
announced to his followers that he was just as talented as
Cortés, maybe more so, and that he was going into business
for himself. This and a few other things caused Cortés
to take a strong hand. He led part of his army across
the uncharted mountains of Mexico and Guatemala, and,
after one of history's most celebrated marches, eventually
made it to Honduras, where he took care of the necessary
housekeeping and planted a colony on the present site of
Puerto Cortés. Dávila's name for the place, Puerto Caballos, seems not to have appealed to Cortés, or perhaps he
had never heard of it. In any case, he called his settlement Natividad de Nuestra Señora—a fine name, admittedly, but one that didn't catch on—and the community
was known as Puerto Caballos until 1859, when it was
rechristened Puerto Cortés. Mariners know it simply as
Cortés.

In company with a dozen members of our crew, I
stepped from the launch onto the dock, near a train of
banana cars, from which our sister ship was being loaded,
and started off down the railroad tracks toward the town.
I knew better than to expect another Lima or Mexico City;
banana ports are not known for public monuments or
other tourist attractions. But it did strike me as strange
that a town that has been continuously inhabited for four
hundred and thirty-three years—forty-one years longer
than St. Augustine, Florida, the oldest settlement in the

United States—should look as if it had been thrown up, any which way, about the same time as Tombstone, Arizona.

There isn't really much of a mystery, however. Economically, Honduras has always been one of the most depressed areas of Central America, and what with yellow fever, malaria, revolutions, dictators, juntas, freebooters, and just plain bad politics, Puerto Cortés has never been very well off. It claims a population in excess of twelve thousand, but I find this figure hard to believe. The count given in most atlases is around seven thousand, and that seems a good deal more plausible. Not that the place couldn't easily accommodate twelve thousand people; including its suburbs, it takes up an area of approximately three square miles. Little of this has been built on, however. Weeds and empty lots abound. Some of the back streets run through the rankest sort of brush, and all the streets are dirt. There are wooden sidewalks on both sides of the main thoroughfare, broken in places and rotting away in others, and the dust between the sidewalks is several inches deep. Except for a small, recently built hotel and the local jail—a stucco structure that used to be the best place for a traveler to spend the night—the town is entirely wooden. Most of the houses have only one story, and many of them, along the waterfront, are built on stilts. Seeming never to have been painted, they all have the pale gray, bleached look that raw lumber takes on after it has baked for years in the sun. Nearly all the roofs are of tin, and nearly all the tin is rusted. I had never seen so much rust anywhere before. It is only a small exaggeration to say that it covers everything—not only the roofs, but every piece of exposed metal; even the heads of the nails in the houses.

The color of rust, as I walked down the railroad tracks with my seafaring companions, gradually began to assert itself as the color of heat. There were other colors to be noticed—the sultry blue of the sky, the grimy yellow of the little railroad station, the green of a small tree laden with a flock of roosting buzzards like loathsome fruit—but all these colors, blue and yellow and green and buzzard, were seen through the bright orange-brown color of rust and heat. Soon I was dripping with sweat. I thought I knew something about heat—the scorched *sertão* of Brazil, the interior of Cuba in July, Times Square during a heat wave —but I couldn't remember any such heat as this.

At the edge of town we came to a side street of bars and other entertaining places, which caused my companions to desert me en masse. I trudged on down the railroad tracks alone, stirring up dust with every step. I tried not to, but it was no use. Puerto Cortés is famous for its dust. I could feel it settling on my skin and into the pair of torn canvas shoes I was wearing. I was glad I had thought to change into them, and into a pair of old, patched drill trousers and a blue cotton shirt. If I had no more sense than to go out in the sun at one o'clock in the afternoon, at least I had sense enough not to overdress.

My immediate objective was the post office. Nobody on the ship had seemed to know quite where it was—one man said it might be next to the new hotel—and when I reached the main street and stepped up onto the wooden sidewalk, which is raised a foot or so above the ground, I looked around for someone who might give me directions. There wasn't a soul to be seen. The sidewalk was shaded here and there by wooden balconies, and in one of the patches of shade a gaunt brown dog with a blunt muzzle was sprawling, fast asleep. I walked past the first shop, a grocery, and then past a barbershop and a one-room hardware store, and all of a sudden it struck me that I had walked past credibility. The grocer was stretched out on his counter, the barber dozed in his chair, and in the hardware store a man and woman, sitting side by side, had their eyes closed and their heads sunk forward on their chests.

Of course, it was only the siesta. Instead of shutting up shop for it, as is the custom in most places where that leisurely tradition prevails, the people of Puerto Cortés simply drop off in their places of business. Others, who have no places of business, simply drop off. Apparently you take your siesta wherever you happen to be. As I continued down the street to the second block, I passed a pool of shade in which three lean, swarthy men were lying, dead to the world. A man with a vast stomach and an enormous mustache sat in a wicker chair before a tailor shop, snoring gently. Near him lay a wrinkled ancient, with one gnarled brown hand trailing over the edge of the sidewalk into the dust.

A block and a half of this, one sleeper after another, and I began to wonder if the heat had done something to my senses. Siesta or no, I said to myself, a whole *town* doesn't go to sleep. It has been a long time since I have read a fairy tale, but it was a fairy tale that came to mind—one of those stories in which an evil magician casts his spell over everybody in sight. If I had discovered at that moment that I was dreaming, I wouldn't have been surprised, but dreaming I was not. In this shop or that, an eye was half opened or a head half raised as I went by—eye and head heavy with lassitude, with the dejection of endless heat—and in a tiny drygoods shop a lovely, dark girl in an immaculate white dress, dozing next to a grandmotherly woman, shook her head complainingly and uttered a few unintelligible words as the boards of the sidewalk creaked beneath my weight. I found myself tiptoeing as I went past.

Puerto Cortés is one of those places where the stores have no front wall (at night, large metal blinds are pulled down), and though I didn't want to stare into the shops—it came too close to prying—I did notice some things. Most of the shops were neat and clean, though their stocks were meager. Practically all the goods were American-made—drugs, razor blades, fountain pens, toilet articles, radios, an electric refrigerator, and one of those frying pans with thermostatic control. Every fifth establishment seemed to be a barbershop. The feature at the movie house was a dubbed-in Spanish version of a twelve-year-old Hollywood film, grade C to begin with, and across the street from the movie house there was a combination lodginghouse and bar that reminded me of those spartan inns that one finds in the villages of Spain. I paused at one of the store fronts long enough to look at a thermometer hung up outside. It was shaded by a balcony, it advertised Coca-Cola, and it said that the temperature was a hundred and two degrees.

At the next intersection, where two men were asleep in the cab of a rusty half-ton truck drawn up near the sidewalk, I came across the first person I had seen on the main street of Puerto Cortés who seemed sufficiently awake to put a question to. He was a short, squat Negro with powerful shoulders and a pock-marked face, and he was sitting on the sidewalk in the shade of another balcony. His eyes were open—half open, anyway—and he raised his head as I approached. I wondered whether he had insomnia or had been awakened by a bad dream. Spanish is one of the politer languages, and I like to think of myself as a polite person, but that man got one of the politest greetings I have ever addressed to anyone, in any language: "Good afternoon, sir. I hesitate to trouble you, but, if you please, will you tell me where the post office is?"

Almost immediately I regretted my intrusion. He looked displeased: he looked almost sullen. Plainly, he objected to being disturbed. He was wearing a pair of black wool trousers, an old-fashioned white shirt without a collar but with a big gold collar button, a black vest, and a pair of heavy shoes. His shoes were covered with dust. He got slowly to his feet, still looking displeased, and pointed down the street. Straight on for three blocks and then a block to the left, he told me—there I would find the post office, next to the new hotel. He mumbled something further, which I did not catch, and then, after I had thanked him, eased himself to his former position on the sidewalk. When I looked back after walking a few feet, his eyes were closed.

The post office, when I got there, was shut up tight, and though I had more than half expected it to be, I felt undone. I could hardly have been dirtier or sweatier, the sun beat down, and I was beginning to be oppressed by the silent, sleeping town. The letters I wanted to mail seemed of absolutely no importance: nothing seemed of any importance except to get out of the heat. There was a square across the street from the post office, and in it, beyond some shrubs splashed with violent red and purple and orange, I saw a circle of palms planted close together, and, inside the circle, unless I was being victimized by a mirage, a pitch-black oasis of shade. I crossed the street and made for it. The shade wasn't a mirage, I was happy to discover, and the square was one of the most attractive I have ever seen.

In its center, and in the center of the circle of palms, grew a huge, wide-spreading tree, with foliage so dense it completely shut out the sky. It looked hundreds of years old. Around the tree, at a radius of about fifty feet from its trunk, a colonnade had been built, its slender pillars holding up a roof of pinkish tiles. The circular space enclosed first by the colonnade and then by the palms was paved with flat, smooth tiles in a pretty blue-and-yellow design. The general effect was that of a roofed-in patio, with the branches and foliage of the tree—which I later learned is known in Honduras as "laurel of India"—forming the roof. I was so grateful for the shade, drinking in such deep draughts of it, that it took me a few minutes to realize I was not alone. Concrete benches stood at regular intervals along the edge of the colonnade. I counted seven benches, and seven men. Each had a bench to himself, and each was fast asleep. Dirtier, raggeder, more abject fellows I have seldom encountered. They were all dressed in those white, or once white, cotton garments that are something of an official uniform for the peon class, and none wore shoes. Travel long enough in the tropics, and your mind works out a sort of mathematics in which poverty is one of the coefficients of heat. I had seen the same kind of thing before, and even worse. This, though, was something different. These men—the companions and inheritors of poverty, the eternally dispossessed—were asleep, helpless and vulnerable, with all their defenses down. The square wasn't for me. I had to be on my way.

Out in the sun again, what I wanted most—what I actually craved—was a beer. My imagination frosted over, brimming with foam. I crossed the street, went past the post office, and entered the hotel. It, too, was asleep. In the otherwise deserted lobby, silent as any tomb, two men were slumped in armchairs—one with his mouth wide open, disclosing a modest fortune in gold teeth, and the other with the Spanish edition of an American picture magazine in his lap. A door led from the lobby into a bar. I could see that the bar was empty, but I went into it anyway; *somebody*, I told myself, had to appear. But no one did. I sat on one of the stools and waited, and I could have been the only man awake—or even alive—on earth. After a few minutes, I couldn't take it any longer. I got myself out of there and walked to the dock through the back part of town. It was dead to the world too. At one intersection I came across a soldier sitting in the dust with his back resting against a tree. He opened his eyes as I went past, but just barely, and then closed them again. He wore battle dress. His rifle lay across his knees, and a cartridge belt, with cartridges, was strapped around his waist. It wasn't until I saw him that I remembered there was trouble in Honduras, with the threat of revolution flickering like heat lightning up in the hills. One manages, I thought to myself: one learns to live with one's time.

My little adventure had lasted about forty-five minutes. When I returned to the dock, my ship was still riding at anchor. The other ship, now loaded, was just casting off. There could be no complaint about lack of life on the dock. A gang of banana carriers—some five hundred of them— had reported for work. It was a rough-looking crowd, and the scene reminded me of one of those movies in which a bandit army takes over a town. Indian types predominated, with a number of Ladinos, or half-castes, mixed in. I saw just a few Negroes and hardly any mulattoes. Though I was the only foreign male on the dock, I was not made conscious of it. In fact, their colloquial greetings and ready companionship gradually brought it home to me that they

assumed I was part of the group. And now that I think of
it, I don't suppose I could have looked more like a banana
carrier if I had tried; I needed a shave, a week at sea had
brought out a lot of old tan, my face was caked with dust
and sweat, my shoes were among the more run-down on
the dock, and my tour of Puerto Cortés had given my
patched trousers and blue cotton shirt a decidedly lived-
in look. I didn't mind my protective coloring. Just as glad
not to be conspicuous, I found a place on a rough wooden
bench where two other men were sitting. They made room
for me in a comradely way and I listened to their talk. I
didn't get all they said—they went too fast—but I gathered
that they had both had bad luck at monte the night before.

Then I noticed two white women sitting on a bench
nearby. One was thin and scrawny—the image that came
to mind was a strip of pemmican—and the other was at
that perilous stage where plumpness is about to get completely out of hand. The first had blue eyes, and straight
black hair caught up in a bun at the nape of her neck. I'm
not very good at guessing ages, but I took her to be in her
late forties. The second was considerably younger. She
had large, slightly protruding gray eyes, with a sort of
stare in them, a hooked nose, and not too generous an
endowment of chin. The women wore cotton dresses, faded
from many launderings, and high-heeled shoes. It seemed
odd that they should be there, two foreign white women
alone in the midst of that bandit army, but, hot and tired
as I was, drained and parched from the effort of my walk,
I don't think I would have paid them any further attention

if the younger one hadn't been shuffling a deck of cards. This was more of an accomplishment than it probably sounds, because a limper, dirtier, more played-out deck of cards I have never seen. It would have been just as easy to shuffle a stack of pancakes.

The women spoke in low voices, almost under their breath, and I couldn't hear what they were saying—not that I cared—but eventually the older one piped up in a louder, more animated tone to call her companion's attention to something or other that was happening aboard the just-loaded vessel as it began to slide away from the dock. There was no mistaking her accent. It was flat as the prairies. You could see the Middle West. Again I wondered briefly what had brought them to this unlikely spot, but then I decided that there was probably some prosaic explanation, and thought about other, happier things—a shave, a shower, a change of clothing, and a long, cool drink. A boy came up, pure Indian, selling small paper cornucopias filled with thin cross sections of banana fried to a crisp. He offered his wares to me as casually as he offered them to my two benchmates. I was still one of the gang. I said no to the boy, as did my companions, and then, as I sat there, my eyes began to close. A moment later, or what seemed to me a moment later, I forced them open again, and when I did I couldn't believe what they saw: my ship, her steam up, appeared to be heading out to sea, and there on the dock, speaking to the women with the deck of cards, was my old friend the Compulsive Traveler.

Or was it? The woman my eyes had fallen upon had the same square bulkiness that I hazily recalled, she wore what could have been the same odds-and-ends costume, and there was the same loose pile of nondescript hair. Even that night in Rio, when I thought I saw her on the streetcar, I hadn't been able to say for sure, and now, after the intervening years, I was even more uncertain—the world is full of square, bulky women with loose piles of nondescript hair.

But suddenly I awakened to what was even more mysterious—and catastrophic. My ship was heading out to sea. Again I wondered whether I could be dreaming, but it was no more a dream than my stroll during the siesta had been. I stared after the ship, asking myself what in the world had happened and waiting for her to turn, but straight down the bay she went, picking up speed. I watched the churning wake she left, and gradually the numbing realization set in—I was stranded in Puerto Cortés. And more than merely stranded. Practically broke as well. I had four dollars and some loose change in my pocket ("Enough for a cable?" I asked myself. "Enough for a night at the inn?"), and as I counted up my assets I was overtaken by the sickening awareness that I had come ashore without any papers—not even the landing card that I was supposed to carry and that no one had asked for. I'm afraid that for a moment my heart sank. I had no name, no nationality, no home, no birthplace, no occupation. I was my own ghost.

What could I do? I could go to the police and tell my

story—but would they believe a word of it? I looked like a tropical tramp. And my four dollars and loose change, American, could easily work against me. My fears raced ahead of my reason. It could be suspected that I had stolen it from one of the sailors who had just left port. I had no proof of anything. I was nobody. Honduras is one of the countries that still require a visa. It doesn't like people without papers, especially during times of revolutionary unrest. I could see myself rotting for months in jail. It wouldn't be the first time a man had disappeared in the tropics.

Ah, but wait a minute—the Compulsive Traveler! She would be able to vouch for me. True, seven years had passed since we were on the boat to Rio, and she probably wouldn't remember me (why should she?), but I could tell her the name of the vessel, the name of the captain, the name of the chief engineer, and the name of the princess. I could even remind her of some of her stories. That should persuade her, surely.

But was it really she? Now that I wanted it to be, I was less certain than ever. I looked hard at her, trying to decide, and my gaze must have been more intense than I realized—she returned my look, and looked a little longer, and then looked through me. What she saw was only too easy to surmise—a renegade white man, most probably a drunkard, sunk into the depths and washed up on the shores of Puerto Cortés. There was no disdain in her look, and no dislike. I was simply a piece of flotsam. There was no way out of it. I would have to give myself up to the authorities.

It didn't work out that way, I'm glad to say. My ship didn't sail off and leave me after all. What had happened was that, in order to tie up properly, she had had to turn around, and, since the channel was too narrow for that, she was obliged to go almost to the end of the bay, a distance of two miles, to make her turn. Once that was accomplished, it was only a matter of fifteen minutes before she was securely moored. I went aboard, had my drink, my shave, and my shower, and then fell asleep. I didn't wake till dinnertime.

After dinner I stood by the rail and watched my old associates of the bandit army at work. They were to be at it all night, and the dock was brilliantly lighted. Trainload after trainload of bananas clattered down to the dock. The fruit was transported in slatted boxcars, similar to those used to freight cattle by rail in the United States. We were to take on forty-eight thousand stems, each of which came from the plantations in a plastic bag, to protect the bananas from bruising.

The carriers were divided into two gangs, of about two hundred and fifty men each. One gang worked the forward hatches, the other the hatches aft. They labored without letup, forming two constantly moving lines. Each man, hoisting a stem of bananas onto his back and shoulders, carried it to a conveyor belt alongside the ship, and the conveyor belt, in turn, carried it down into the hold.

It is hard work to budge a stem of bananas, let alone carry one, but the loaders had developed such a technique that quite a few of them weren't even perspiring. However, they all faced a hazard that I wouldn't much care to encounter. When the banana bunch is cut from the tree, a sizable part of its long, tough stem is left on; this length of stem, protruding from the mouth of the plastic bag, gives the loaders something to grab hold of. The difficulty is that the bunches can't be conveniently fitted into the hold of a ship with that much stem, so at the dock most of it must be lopped off. This task is assigned to one of the workers. Armed with a machete, he stands midway between the railroad cars and the conveyor belt assigned to his gang. As each carrier passes before him, he makes a single swipe with his machete, the razor-sharp blade coming within inches of the poor fellow bent under his load, and—slash!—off comes the stem. It's an unnerving process to watch, but the carriers seemed to deliver themselves up to the men with the machetes without any fear. These experts are so skilled that with their stroke, finished off with a quick snap of the wrist, they can usually send the severed stem flying straight into a bushel basket kept there for the purpose. Each basket is attended by another worker, who scrambles for the stems that go wide of the mark. Not many do. I kept score on one of the machete-wielders, and he hit the basket forty-two times out of fifty.

On toward eight o'clock, in what could pass for the cool of the evening, I decided to have another turn around the town. I wanted to see what it was like at night, and, besides, I thought I might be lucky enough to get another look at the woman I believed to be my fellow voyager to Rio. Down on the dock, the captain of our ship, a barnacled veteran named Grant, was talking with the two women I had seen when I returned from my afternoon stroll. They had apparently been on the dock ever since. I joined the group and found the women a curious pair. According to their story, told by the one with the Midwestern accent (she was from Ohio, it turned out), they were fortune-tellers. She said that her companion had studied with the gypsies. They had told fortunes all through Nicaragua and Guatemala and were now trying to tell enough fortunes in Puerto Cortés to get back to the United States. A yarn like that would be good enough for a touch any day, even without a price of soothsaying thrown in, but I had my fortune told (within two weeks I was going to meet a ravishing heiress who would lead me into all kinds of interesting mischief, and here I am, getting gray still waiting), and after that I asked about the Compulsive Traveler—or the woman I had taken for her.

The fortunetellers recalled her saying that she had recently spent a day in Guatemala City and that she had also visited Tegucigalpa, the Honduran capital. What she was doing in Puerto Cortés they didn't know. She hadn't said and they hadn't asked. They remembered that she had watched the earlier part of the banana loading and had left the dock just before dark. They imagined that she might be at the hotel.

She wasn't, though. That much I can be positive about

because I went to the hotel and inquired. The clerk told me that he didn't have a lady registered and hadn't had for weeks. He remarked that there was the inn, of course, but that it would be useless for me to look for a lady there, since the inn catered only to a male clientele. Very rough. Very noisy. Sometimes fights. An unthinkable place for a lady.

Leaving the hotel, I wandered around the town. Puerto Cortés at night bore little resemblance to Puerto Cortés at siesta time. Whoever it is in the fairy tale who overcomes the wicked magician and liberates the bewitched town had been on the job. The stores were busy, the bars were full, and knots of men sat crowded together on the wooden sidewalks, playing cards. Everywhere I went, I kept a sharp lookout for that loose pile of nondescript hair. I had no luck, however, and after an hour or so I decided to give up. But just before returning to my ship I went back to the hotel. I still had my letters to mail, shoved into one of my pockets, and I had thought of a question I wanted to ask.

The clerk, a thin-faced man in white trousers and a white shirt, seemed rather surprised to see me again. He was extremely sympathetic and most anxious to help. He was so sympathetic and anxious to help that gradually it dawned on me what he was thinking—that I had arranged a date in his hotel and had been stood up. He said that he would be glad to post my letters, and then, getting around to the question I wanted to ask, I inquired if there had been any passenger trains out of Puerto Cortés that afternoon. There hadn't been any since early morning, he told me; however, a bus—privately owned but most dependable—was due to leave at ten o'clock that evening for San Pedro Sula, fifty miles inland. There was an airport in San Pedro Sula, he said, and from there one could arrange to go anywhere.

The more I thought about it, the more easily I was able to persuade myself that it was the Compulsive Traveler I had met up with. Everything hung together—the bit I got from the fortunetellers about Guatemala City and Tegucigalpa, the fact that she never stayed in one place for any length of time, and now the bus to San Pedro Sula. The clock over the hotel desk said a few minutes before ten. I asked the clerk where I might find the bus station and was told that there was no bus station. He explained that the bus made two stops in Puerto Cortés to pick up passengers—one in the main part of town, near a bar, and the other at a corner of the square just across the street. The bus should be coming along any minute, he said.

Bidding the clerk what I suspect he hoped was a final good night, I crossed over to the square. A radio was going full blast with something noisy on a marimba—free entertainment provided by the town fathers—and the square, like the rest of Puerto Cortés, had been released from its spell. It was lighted by street lamps along all four sides, and in its patiolike center, where the big laurel of India grew, there was a string of electric bulbs. More women than men were in evidence, which was hardly surprising

in view of the convocation of cardplayers on the sidewalks and the gang of workers loading bananas. Babies
crawled around. Some well-behaved teen-agers were
dancing on the tiles. Young men and young women visited
with each other discreetly. Vendors strolled around with
baskets. The radio stopped, took a deep breath, and
started up again. This time it gave out with "La Giralda,"
one of the *paso dobles* played at bullfights. There isn't a
bull ring in all of Honduras, but somebody in the control
room must have been wishing there was.

It was in the middle of "La Giralda" that I realized the
bus had arrived. I was so interested in the little fiesta that
I hadn't seen it drive up. The sound of its horn was what
attracted my attention. It was a Volkswagen bus, and the
driver had pulled up at the corner nearest me, right under
a lamppost. Only one passenger was preparing to board—a
thin Indian woman, dressed all in black, who had a tense,
burning look concentrated between high, gaunt cheekbones. She was carrying an infant, a basket, and a large
parcel wrapped in newspaper. Standing on the sidewalk,
I could easily see into the bus. I looked, and there, sitting
by one of the open windows, was the Compulsive Traveler.
But was it, really? I stood not six feet away from her. She
peered out the window through her steel-rimmed spectacles, seeing what was to be seen, and then, no longer interested, picked up a long, stringy piece of knitting from her
lap. I remembered another long, stringy piece of knitting
carried about everywhere, and it was the knitting that
finally did it—the knitting, and one thing more.

She must have felt my eyes on her. She looked up from her knitting, and the motion of her head, quick and jerky, gave an impression of impatience. It was exactly the same motion I recalled from the time my shadow fell across her work when we were on the boat to Rio. I couldn't possibly be mistaken. Now I was sure. The Compulsive Traveler had been having a look at Puerto Cortés.

Our glances held for an instant, and then, feeling companionable, I ventured a smile. She didn't smile back. She looked at me an instant longer, however, and the expression on her face—puzzled, almost worried—made it seem that she was trying to recall where she had seen me before. I would have gone up and explained everything if, at that moment, the bus hadn't left. It drove off just as "La Giralda" came to an end. I watched the small red glow of its taillights until they disappeared, wondering where my old friend was off to this time. Ecuador? Finland? Vietnam? Anybody's guess is as good as mine.

Jamaica Journal

JAMAICA JOURNAL

THE worst drawback to air transportation, as I see it, is
that it saves too much time. There is no room for prepara-
tion and adjustment, no gradual introduction to a different place and scene. Here I am over the interior of Cuba,
with the island of Jamaica an hour ahead, and my mind
is still full of the United States. I can understand walking,
and after forty years I am beginning to understand the
automobile, but flying introduces a new dimension I cannot grasp. It is all very well for me to be told that London
and Paris are now only a few hours away, as in terms of
flight I know they are, but these are not the terms of my
everyday experience. I never think of London and Paris
as being only a few hours away, and it would never occur
to me to call up a friend in either place to say that I will
be dropping in shortly for a drink. However, according to
the flight steward who has just handed me a customs form
to fill out, it seems that I will soon be dropping in on Jamaica. My every tendency is to resist the idea—it even
annoys me a little—but I suppose it is true.

Even though I have seen blue water before—the Gulf
Stream; the Mediterranean; the Gulf of Mexico—these
waters of the Caribbean seem blue enough to stain. One
of the questions asked on the customs form is do I have

any opium in my possession, and if so how much? The trouble here is that I am as antagonistic to forms as I am opposed to opium. I assume that there must be a reason for the question, since the rest of the form doesn't suggest an exactly playful imagination, but to me this is another reminder that there is a nearer worry than the next ice age. Let the present drift continue, and the whole earth from pole to pole is going to be buried under a blanket of forms a hundred feet deep. It may interest some archaeologist from another planet to learn that in the month of March 1950, when I went to Jamaica for a visit of six weeks, I had no opium to declare.

Our hostess is one of those attractive, competent young women on whom the airlines seem to have a monopoly. A few minutes ago she joined me for a visit. She told me that she was born and raised in Glendale, California, and that this is her first job. When I asked her why she chose it— if she was interested in aviation or travel—she said good gracious no, she would rather have a stay-at-home job in Glendale any day. Apparently sensing my mystification, she went on to explain that she had majored in languages at college and had then gone on to study Spanish at the University of Mexico. Not wanting to teach the language, which she said was all that her education had fitted her for, she decided to get into airlining. "Unless I married a Mexican," she said, "this was the only way I could get to use my Spanish."

Still not sure that I understood her line of reasoning, but

willing to go along, I suggested that perhaps she could have been a bullfighter—I mentioned a lady *torero* I had been reading about, and she shook her head seriously. "That girl speaks hardly a word of Spanish," she said with just a trace of severity. "I wanted really to *use* it." I went back over the steps of her logic (she was disinclined to teach, marry a Mexican, or be a bullfighter, but wanted to use her Spanish) and found it flawless except for one thing. Other than to say a few words over the plane's loudspeaker, explaining that this is the flight from Miami, Florida, to Barranquilla, Colombia, and to answer the infrequent questions of such Spanish-speaking persons who may be aboard, her Spanish doesn't get much of a workout. "And besides all that, I like Spanish food," she added. "I got to like it when I was in Mexico, and there is a good little restaurant in Barranquilla." For me that settled it. Add a liking for Spanish food to not wanting to teach, marry a Mexican, or be a bullfighter—*plus* a good little restaurant in Barranquilla—and why shouldn't a girl make airlining her career?

Left to my own devices, I peered from the window. We came to a dense mass of cloud and climbed above it into the sun. We have now reached that stage of the journey when the steady drone of the motors has brought everyone to the verge of sleep. A few of the passengers, gone over the edge, are snoring peacefully. Another accumulation of cloud, a gradual descent, and then, through a break in the mist, a sudden landfall ahead. Jamaica, B.W.I. A broken shoreline indented by little coves, blue blue water spangled with sunlight, and a ridge of mountains against the sky. As we bank, preparing to land, I am able to get a better look. The green of the trees is a darker, more secret green than is ever to be found in the temperate regions, the sunlight is brighter and less filtered, the reds and yellows and oranges of the flowers are more emphatic and sultry—the plane comes to a stop, the door is opened, and the flat, still heat of the tropics is mixed with the smell of cane.

Jamaica arrived on the world scene with Christopher Columbus. One of the Greater Antilles, it is one hundred and forty-eight miles long, fifty-two miles across at its greatest width, and twenty-two and a half miles at its narrowest. Lying ninety miles south of Cuba, it is one hundred miles west of Haiti and three hundred and ten miles from Cape Gracias on the eastern coast of Honduras, the nearest point of the American continent. It is one of the more mountainous of the Caribbean islands, and some of its peaks, notably those of the Blue Mountains, rise to heights of from four thousand to seven thousand feet. It is watered by over a hundred rivers and streams. Only a few of these are navigable, however, and none are used as avenues of trade. Kingston is the capital and chief port. Other harbors are Port Morant, Old Harbour, Dry Harbour, Montego Bay, St. Ann's Bay, Port Maria, and Port Antonio.

Columbus did not reach Jamaica until his second voyage. He discovered it on May 3, 1494. Just where he landed is a matter of dispute, but most authorities believe it was on the north shore of the island, at a place designated on the map as Dry Harbour. Sometimes it is called Discovery Bay. Columbus christened his new island Santiago, but the name by which it is thought to have been known to the Arawak Indians he found there—Xaymaca—has managed to survive. The meaning of the word is also disputed. Some scholars hold it to signify "land of wood and water," others "island of springs," and still others simply "well-watered."

The Arawak Indians that the Spaniards found in Jamaica are now among the world's lost peoples. "Of at least 60,000 souls found on the island," wrote one historian, "not a single descendant existed when Penn and Venables captured it for the British. A whole people had been exterminated." Beyond this accomplishment, the Spaniards left but little impress on Jamaica. The story of their stewardship, which lasted for a century and a half, is summed up by the population figures for 1655, when Penn and Venables launched their invasion—no more Arawaks, fifteen hundred Spaniards, and approximately two thousand Negro slaves brought from Africa.

Penn and Venables were Cromwell's men, Penn an admiral and Venables a general. Convinced that Spain was England's natural enemy, "the underpropper of Babylon," and committed to the English position that Spain's claim to the West Indies by virtue of a papal bull was invalid, Cromwell sent Penn and Venables on an expedition to the Caribbean. Its purpose was to capture Cuba and Hispaniola. Penn's and Venables' purpose appears to have been to annoy each other; rarely have two commanders been on such bad terms. Making a fiasco of the attack on Hispaniola, they found it convenient to ignore Cuba and turned their attention to Jamaica instead. Taken by surprise, the Spaniards speedily capitulated. Jamaica was a fairly insignificant prize compared with Cuba and Hispaniola, but it had the distinction of being the first British colony to be taken by force, and has ever since remained the largest and most important possession of the Crown in the West Indies. The population of the island is approximately one and one third million, of which ninety-eight per cent is black.

The Engishmen who have figured in the history of Jamaica make a notable list. Henry Morgan, the pirate's pirate who went respectable, was one of its first lieutenant governors. The novelist Smollett lived on the island in the mid-1700's, when he was a surgeon's mate in the Royal Navy, and married the daughter of a Jamaican planter. Horatio Nelson almost perished of malaria here in 1778. Captain William Bligh, on a voyage undertaken after his experiences on the *Bounty*, arrived in 1793 with a boatload of trees and plants from the South Seas, and the variety of mango known locally as "Number Seven" was so named because it was in the seventh box that Bligh loaded in Tahiti and caused to be labeled with that number in black paint. Matthew Gregory Lewis, better remembered as Monk Lewis from the title of his most famous book, "The Monk," owned several Jamaican estates, which he visited in 1816 and 1818, and told of his experiences in what is perhaps the best volume ever written about the island, "Journal of a West Indian Proprietor." Lewis died ten days out of Jamaica on a sloop bound for London, in the arms of his valet Tita. This was the same Tita who later was employed by Byron and was present at the poet's death.

Intriguing as these names are, I find the place names of Jamaica hardly less so. The Arawaks, the Spaniards, and the British each left their mark on the map. Among the few surviving names of Arawak origin are Mammee Bay ("mammee," pronounced "mammy," is the name of a fruit tree), Mammee Gulley, and Mammee Ridge. The Spanish occupation is recalled by the names of some of the rivers—Rio Alto (Deep River); Rio Cobre (Copper River); Rio D'Oro (Golden River)—and there are other Spanish names that have been so corrupted that they are no longer recognizable. Boca de Agua, for instance, or "Water's Mouth," is now Bog Walk; and Agua Alta Bahia, which translates into "Deep Water Bay," has become Wag Water. The British showed their usual fondness for hills (Cut Throat Hill, May Day Hill, Pimento Hill); halls (Amity Hall, Unity Hall, Harmony Hall); and castles (Blue Castle, Stirling Castle, Dublin Castle). But it is names like the following that leap to the eye—Doona Dump, Poorthing, Wait-a-bit, Happy Hut, Bold Attempt, Starve Gut Bay, Welsh Woman's Point, Turtle Crawl Harbour, Heirs of Tharp, God Almighty's Cut Stones, Dog Gully, Ben Grung, Kin Owl, Fly-tox Alley, and Ackee Walk. I have been told that there is a calypso song made up of some of these names, and I'm not surprised. The possibilities are endless.

Kingston, Jamaica's capital and largest community, has a population of approximately one hundred and forty thousand, and the whole population seems always to be on the streets during daylight hours at the same time—men and women on foot, making use of their heads to carry anything from a single ripe tomato to a ten-foot log; other men and women on bicycles and donkeys; swarms of little boys; solitary little girls; vendors; automobiles and lorries of various makes and vintages; now and then a cow; frequently a goat; sometimes a pig; more often a horse and wagon; and on every corner a knot of chatting, laughing, quarreling people who apparently have an intense aversion to shade and prefer to conduct all their affairs in the sun. Passing a shopwindow, I caught the reflection of a white face amid all the black ones—bleached out and alien, solemn and preoccupied—and it took me an instant to recognize it as my own.

The Kingston Flower Market—What I thought of was tubes of pigment, reds and yellows and oranges and greens and blues, tied together like a string of firecrackers and then set off all at once, the explosions hanging fixed and motionless in the air. Walking past the flower market, and strolling aimlessly, I found myself in a teeming, wholly native section known as Cheapside, where part of the sidewalk is used to display all kinds of broken-down merchandise. Coming as I do from an economy predicated on waste, and the more waste the better, since by our wastefulness we keep turning the wheels that supply us with the new, improved models of the things we have been urged to waste; automobiles especially, but not only automobiles; refrigerators and washing machines and lawn mowers and almost anything that can be named, even New York sky-scrapers—living in such a climate, I am forever being struck anew by the circumstance that there are some parts of the world (not some parts: most parts) where even so common-place an article as a glass bottle, a broomstick, or a door-knob is expected to last as long as the material from which it is made, and retains some fractional part of its original value until the very end.

Nor do I have in mind the flea and thieves' markets of Europe—compared with the debris of Cheapside, those are princely displays. *Items:* A bashed-in pail; a teakettle with-out a spout; a handful of nails, mostly bent; the blade of a hoe; two rusty five-gallon tins; five small bottles that once contained patent medicine; a pile of larger bottles, various shapes and sizes; a saucepan with a crooked handle; a chipped chamber pot; five saucers and four cups, three of the saucers and two of the cups being cracked; a mason's trowel pebbly with cement; the head of a hammer; the shaft of an ax, split at one end; half of a whetstone; a chisel with a broken edge; a pair of automobile tires worn to the webbing; a twisted bicycle wheel, minus most of its spokes; two coal-oil lamps needing wicks; four tin spoons; a celluloid collar full of stains; a misshapen hat with a purple feather; a pair of yellow dancing slippers, both heels gone— *Junk!* one thinks, having been conditioned by a wholly different mercantile experience, and it seems incredible that any of this litter, this junk, could be of value or ever be sold.

But it is of value and it is sold. There are few places in Kingston where trade is brisker than at the Cheapside market. I watched the boisterous haggling for a time—a woman paying tuppence for the yellow dancing slippers; a man handing over a shilling for the two five-gallon tins —and then continued down the street. I had not walked far, not more than two or three blocks, when I stopped again. What brought me to a halt was a cluster of hovels, fifty or more, put together out of palm leaves, pasteboard cartons, tin cans pounded flat, scraps of tar paper, and rotting bits of lumber. Of all the slums I have happened to come upon, this was the very worst. It stands in the midst of a dump that many years ago used to be a graveyard— the air thick with the smell of garbage and alive with the hum of carrion flies—and because the dump is supposed to be haunted by the ghosts, or "duppies," of those who are buried there, the slum is known as Duppy Town. But no prevalence of duppies could be more fearsome than the creatures who now inhabit the place—hairy, bearded, wild-looking men who go about in filthy rags.

They call themselves the Rastafari. Looking upon Emperor Haile Selassie of Ethiopia as their lord, master, and rightful sovereign, they hold themselves aloof from all other Jamaicans, regardless of color. They believe that

Haile Selassie will summon them to his kingdom someday, and that, when he does, their beards will cause the waters to part and they will walk to Africa dry-shod. Beyond this, not much is known about them. I was told that they are not a religious sect, though some of them are supposed to be witch doctors, and why they have pledged their loyalty to Haile Selassie is a mystery. They have never been known to work, or even to beg. They are said to keep alive by scavenging the dump, disposing of their plunder at the Cheapside market, and by various forms of petty thievery. There isn't a soul in Kingston who will walk past their settlement at night, and it is generally avoided even by day. I didn't linger long. Something told me I was out of bounds.

The ruling clan of Kingston, and the most powerful home-grown dynasty in the Caribbean, is a family that has its origins in the Middle East, a father and two sons. Each is reputed to be a millionaire many times over. But what I heard stressed in social conversation wherever I went was not their wealth but the vise-like terror of the father's handshake—there were visitors from as far away as Liverpool and Seattle, Hong Kong and Karachi, who had had to grit their teeth. Be careful, I was warned. That handshake would leave me crippled for days.

When I met the gentleman I found him to be a short, husky, grizzled man in his late seventies, bearing on his features the stamp of the Levant and built along the lines of an Angus bull. We shook hands, which left me not quite crippled, and I mused upon the advantages of being a member of a small, relatively self-contained society—James Boswell made a reputation by going to Corsica and interviewing General Paoli, Patrick Henry became famous by virtue of a single line, and here in Jamaica the blacksmith's grip of this low-slung grandfather has created a legend that has been carried across seas and continents and will outlive him by years. And the thing is that he loves it. Let the choice be put to him—give up your riches or your handshake—and I wouldn't be surprised if he decided to surrender the former. As a man of millions he is one among many. His identity is his handshake. "Most men won't shake hands with me," he said. "They're afraid to."

My acquaintance R, an Englishman of some means and position who came out to Jamaica thirty years ago, asked me to have a drink. "Sometimes I stand back and take a good look at myself and wonder what I'm doing here," he said. "This island is a backwash, don't you know, and Kingston has all the drawbacks of a provincial town. I know you, and you know the next man, and everything one says is repeated. I don't like being here, not really, and yet I'll stay. I'll always stay. There is only one explanation I can offer. Years ago, when I was a boy in England, I read a poem, 'The Spell of the Tropics.' I don't remember who wrote it, or what the lines were, or anything about it except the title. And yet it was that poem that brought me here—it held up something: a vision, you might say—and it is because of that poem that I'll stay. But it's a curious thing, don't you know. I quite dislike poetry and always have, even as a boy."

A cruise ship put in this morning for a one-day stay, loaded to the gunwales with various American types, and all day long they have been roaming the streets of Kingston in funny hats. Now it is sunset and the vessel is preparing to sail. Several hundred natives have gathered on the docks, which are only three blocks from my hotel, and for the past hour they have been singing in unison. The hope is that they will be thrown a few coins by the departing vacationists. At first the singing was fairly subdued and disciplined, not unlike that of a massed choir. Gradually it mounted in volume, maintaining a steady insistent chant that depends on the monotonous reiteration of two notes and sounds something like *yo LA/ yo LA*, against which the voices of individual singers began to rise and fall. Slowly the volume increased, the beat of the chant getting faster and faster and more and more soloists making themselves heard, until now, working on itself and feeding on itself, the accumulation of sound has mounted to a wild, orgiastic frenzy. Sitting in my hotel room, I can feel the impact. Without being there I can tell that things are getting out of hand. Perhaps the cruise people are entertained, but I'm not—that everlasting *yo LA/ yo LA*, like the ceaseless beating of a drum, crisscrossed by long, quavering wails, is doing things to my nerves. No longer does this bear any resemblance to singing. It has become the outpouring of a whole set of emotions, attitudes, and buried secrets I cannot hope to understand, and by which, because of my ignorance, and in some atavistic way I am unable to explain, I feel vaguely threatened. I have always thought that Eugene O'Neill muffed it in "The Emperor Jones," which has to be seen as essentially the work of a sophomoric imagination, but I now realize that he was on the right track.

Calypso is just beginning to be heard in the United States,[1] but here in Jamaica it is hard to get away from. For me its appeal is limited. I find the music repetitious as a dentist's drill, and the bawdy verses that accompany so much of it are to my mind much less entertaining than such hairy-eared ballads as "The Fly Flew into the Grocery Shop" and the rowdy backwoods version of "She'll Be Coming 'round the Mountain."

Why is it called calypso? Nobody seems to know. That the word as applied to these basically African rhythms has

[1] I am letting this stand as it was written, before calypso became a world-wide vogue. And perhaps it should be mentioned that the *chiqué* Jamaica of the present time, whose expense-account atmosphere would seem to have been captured in a series of recent advertisements—an aging actor-playwright posing in red shoes on some rocks in the surf; a comic poultryman in no shoes at all preparing to attack a grand piano on the beach; a fading musical-comedy star leaping across the sands; a ubiquitous conductor sitting in the front row of a native band—this Jamaica, so fast has time and tourism moved, bears but little resemblance to the far from undiscovered, but still relatively authentic, Jamaica of only ten years ago. To go back any farther than that—to the decade just before the Second World War, for instance—would be to stack the cards.

any connection with the Calypso of the Ulysses story, the queen of the island of Ogygia, on whose shores Ulysses was shipwrecked and remained for seven years, Calypso perishing of sorrow when he finally departed, would appear to be so unlikely as to preclude serious consideration. A faintly more plausible theory might be built up on the basis of what some scholars hold to be the meaning of the name Calypso, "The Hidden One," since there are some calypso songs that are said to have a submerged meaning known only to the natives. Such a theory, however, would have to presuppose a rather intimate knowledge of Greek on the part of a people who in the mass are functionally illiterate, and in addition it would have to overlook the fact that much of the calypso one hears in these parts is about as submerged as Pikes Peak.

I am thinking specifically of a song called "Janie," to which I was introduced last night. Some hospitable Kingston people invited me to supper, and then later we joined a party at an open-air night club called "The Glass Bucket." I was seated next to a fair, blond young Englishwoman from Devonshire, a Mrs. G, who, with her husband, has been living in Jamaica for the past several years. Three strolling minstrels were part of the entertainment at the night club, going from table to table when the band took an intermission. One played a guitar, the other rattled a pair of gourds, and the third kept time with a pair of mahogany sticks. Eventually they came to our table and began to sing "Janie." The first stanza was harmless enough:

> *When me look on me Janie gal*
> *Water come a me eyes*
> *When me look on me Janie gal*
> *Water come a me eyes*

and the refrain was pitched on the same innocent, simple-minded level:

> *Come back Janie*
> *Come back gal*
> *Water come a me eyes*
> *Come back Janie*
> *Come back gal*
> *Water come a me eyes*

So far so good. Mrs. G sat listening, as attentive as if she were at a concert in Covent Garden, her chin resting on the back of one hand. The next stanza fell upon our ears:

> *When me look on me Janie's belly*
> *Water come a me eyes*
> *When me look on me Janie's belly*
> *Water come a me eyes*

And from then on, for at least six times round, the various parts of Janie's anatomy were no less pointedly looked at fore and aft, each part being given its precise, low-life designation. Not once did Mrs. G's expression change. Her black lace dress emphasized her fair Devonshire poise. When finally the survey of Janie was completed and the trio had moved on, she leaned toward me. She said, "I haven't heard much of this Jamaica calypso. It's rather interesting, don't you think?" and for a moment I was unable to answer. Nor was it in my mind to disagree. What had rendered me mute was that I had never been so admiring of British aplomb.

Fifteen miles from Kingston, at the tip of a long, narrow peninsula, stands the town of Port Royal—a dull and uninteresting settlement that in its day was the most famous place in the New World. For this is the Port Royal of pirate fame. It was here that Henry Morgan and other buccaneers used to return with the plunder of the Spanish galleons, along with the loot taken on their quick, bloody raids upon Cartagena, Puerto Rico, and Hispaniola. "The City of Gold," it was called, "The Shame of the West," and when the larger part of it was tumbled into the sea by an earthquake in 1692, one of nature's epic disasters, the tremor was felt as far away as London and Madrid. Except for a brick fort built by the British a few years before the catastrophe, nothing remains of the old town.

I was pleased to learn that the pirates are still remembered in their former country. A gray-haired Negro fisherman with whom I fell into conversation pointed out a low-lying key that shimmered a few hundred yards offshore, and explained that it was there that Morgan hanged the more troublesome of his former associates after he became lieutenant governor and had to keep the peace. And a lively boy of twelve, shiny black, told me how it was when the streets of Port Royal were heaped with bales of silk, satin, and velvet, and even mounds of gold. His eyes grew

big as he spoke, as if he could see the booty spread
out before him. "But it was a wicked city, sir," he concluded
gravely. "A very wicked city. That is why God sent the
earthquake and had it swallowed by the sea. The preacher
man has said so, many times." Walking on alone, I thought
what a fortunate preacher man he was. Even the thunder-
ers of the Old Testament rarely found such apt material
so close at hand.

It is part of Jamaican folklore that the ruins of Port
Royal may be seen at the bottom of the sea on a clear day.
I have yet to meet anyone who has gazed on this wonder or
who knows anyone who has, but the story persists. And
a good thing too, I believe. A place wants ghosts—witness
the difference between Milan and Milwaukee—and what
better incentive to song and story than a lost drowned
city? To be persuaded, we need only remember a piece of
music by Debussy. One of the ghostlier Port Royal legends
is that once upon a time the bell in the submerged cathedral could be heard beneath the waters as it was swayed
to and fro by the tide. This gave Debussy the idea for *La
Cathédrale Engloutie.*

The fort at Port Royal is where Horatio Nelson almost
died of malaria when he was stationed in Jamaica. His
former quarters are still to be seen, and there is a long
wooden platform, running the length of the rampart and
overlooking the sea, on which he is said to have taken his
daily exercise—"Nelson's quarter-deck," it is called. Over

one of the arches that give entrance to the fort is a marble tablet bearing this inscription: "In This Place Dwelt Horatio Nelson. You Who Tread His Footsteps Remember His Glory."

But Nelson's local glory is kept green in a livelier fashion. Imbedded in the outer facing of the walls of the fort are three small white crosses—the Negro guide pointed them out to me. "This one is Mary, this one is Lucy, and this one is Jane," he said. "They were three young ladies who followed Nelson out from England and became his sweethearts while he was here, all at the same time. When he had to return to England he thought it might make trouble for him—three sweethearts at the same time—so he had them shot. He ordered them buried in unmarked graves, with just those three crosses, but that's who they were— Mary, Lucy, and Jane." I started to laugh and then checked myself; the man was serious as an owl. And I find the story is widely believed in Port Royal, and to a lesser extent in Kingston. Nothing will ever convince some of these people that Horatio Nelson didn't cause three young Englishwomen to be murdered in cold blood.

Now I am in a place called Tryall, on the north shore of the island, a few miles from Montego Bay. Though most people make the same trip by car from Kingston in a few hours, it took me two days. I was in no hurry, however, and enjoyed loafing along. I left Kingston on a Sunday morning in a small English automobile I had rented, and my first stop was Spanish Town, thirteen miles from Kingston on a good paved road. Spanish Town was St. Jaga de la Vega (St. James of the Plain) originally. The Spaniards laid it out in 1520, and it was their capital city. The British also made it their capital until the seat of government was transferred to Kingston in 1872.

Jamaica hasn't had much luck with its older buildings. What was left of Port Royal after the earthquake of 1692 was destroyed by a fire in 1703. The prints and engravings of Kingston a hundred years ago make it appear to have been an extremely attractive place, with simple, indigenous houses designed by local amateurs without formal architectural training, but all that remains of that Kingston is the street plan. It too was leveled by an earthquake, this one in 1907, and then was further damaged, over a span of years, by any number of scattered fires. So as a result, the finest group of buildings in Jamaica—which is another way of saying the finest group of buildings anywhere in the British possessions in the West Indies—are those that face the square in Spanish Town.

The square itself is a pleasant place, with a little fountain and a wrought-iron picket fence that give it a vaguely Spanish look, but if it were not for its buildings, it wouldn't be worth a second glance. There are four structures in all, each occupying a side of the square—the old Governor's Mansion (King's House) on the west, the former House of Assembly on the east, the Courts of Justice on the south, and the Rodney Memorial[2] on the north. They would be

---

[2] Admiral George Brydges Rodney (1719–92) was in command of an English fleet that won a decisive victory over the French off the island of Dominica in 1782, saving Jamaica from possible capture.

impressive anywhere—white, pure Georgian, dating from the mid- and late 1700's—but to come upon them without forewarning, in that dusty forgotten place and in the stillness of a Sunday morning, was altogether astonishing.

King's House, the largest and most imposing of the group, was once the most admired building in the English-speaking part of the New World—"the noblest and best edifice of its kind, either in North America or any of the British Colonies in the West Indies." To me, though, the prize of the place is the Rodney Memorial. I doubt that there is a finer example of the late Georgian style anywhere. The structure consists of a pair of two-story wings, each making a corner of the block, which are connected by a colonnaded arcade. Set back on a curve from the sidewalk, the colonnade is broken in its center by a lavishly ornamented baroque canopy that houses a statue of Rodney, and the canopy is roofed over by a dome that is topped off, almost frivolously, with a cupola in the form of a miniature Greek temple. I have been trying to learn who the architect was, but so far have been unable to turn up a single clue. Two things, however, are certain—he was no amateur, and in this instance he was touched with genius. Nothing he tried went wrong.

(*I did not know, when I was in Spanish Town, that it links up with the American Revolution, as is explained in E. Arnot Robertson's "The Spanish Town Papers" [Macmillan, 1959]. The papers referred to are nearly a thousand bundles of ships' papers, each parcel containing various documents taken from American vessels captured in the South Atlantic or the Caribbean during the*

*War of Independence, and then brought to the British
naval base at Port Royal. The papers found on them—log-
books, love letters, family correspondence—were left for a
hundred and twenty years after the war ended to molder
and decay in the Old Court House in Harbour Street,
Kingston. This was one of the buildings destroyed by the
earthquake of 1907. Some of the documents were salvaged,
others were lost. When Miss Robertson and her husband
discovered them twenty years ago, they had been depos-
ited in Spanish Town. The temptation to quote from the
papers is enormous, but not even extensive quotation
would convey their quality, drama, and interest.)*

Just past Spanish Town, the cane fields begin. Even
though it was Sunday, men and women were working at
getting in the crop. The men were cutting the cane with
machetes (an all-purpose tool in Jamaica: one afternoon
in Kingston I watched a burly fellow trimming a friend's
hair with one), and the women were loading it in high,
trough-shaped carts with wooden wheels. Back in the
1870's, the cane fields all over the island were alive with
rats. Somebody thought of importing the mongoose to get
rid of them. Which the mongoose was glad to do. Then the
little animals made a sweep of all the snakes. Since none of
the snakes was poisonous, this was a dubious accomplishment. Next the poultry was got after, and now the mongoose is nobody's friend. Multiplying into the thousands,
the benefactor has become a pest. One sees the creatures
everywhere, scurrying through the fields and darting

across the roads, and over every dead form the natives re-
joice. I have been told by three of them that the mongoose
was introduced by a retired colonel who had served in
India. It is impossible to verify the story, which is much too
pat, anyway, but I am getting the notion that in native
circles the mongoose represents a flagrant example of colo-
nial misrule.

Jamaica is a well-roaded island, and all the roads are
clearly posted. There was no reason for me to get lost on
my way to Montego Bay, but I did. And what caused me
to go astray, I have decided, was the sisal I saw in bloom.
I came upon it just beyond Mandeville, a town in the hills
where I spent the night. The sisal had grown to a height of
more than thirty feet and was in full bloom, and its fan-
like crown of massed orange-yellow blossoms had attracted
a flock of hummingbirds. Most belonged to the familiar
ruby-throat family, others were a blackish, metallic green,
and one handsome fellow, with a jet-black crest, had two
very long, very black tail feathers that streamed like ribbons when he flew.

It was a few miles later that I took a wrong turning. And
then, as I got deeper and deeper into the back country, my
sense of direction was further blunted by the number of
trees that were in flower—poincianas, spathodias, immor-
telles, ackees laden with bright red fruit, and wild oranges
everywhere. In my lack of attention, I lost my way completely. It wasn't until midafternoon, however, after I had
eaten a few sandwiches that I brought with me from

Mandeville, that I began to realize what had happened. I had no idea where I was and couldn't find a signpost anywhere. I could think of nothing better to do than to follow the road I had been traveling—a mere wagon track deep with ruts that must have been there since last year's rains—and hope that it would lead to some village where I could get my bearings.

But where it led, instead, was into a solid jungle of bamboo. The wagon track dwindled into a barely defined footpath just wide enough to accommodate my car. And it was then, as sunset was approaching and I was beginning to get uneasy, that a small, slight, almost wispy Negro came into view, leading a brown-and-white cow. He wore a patched blue shirt, dark trousers, a gray cap, and a pair of heavy brogans. Apparently sensing that I was in some sort of difficulty, he led his cow to my car. He listened sympathetically as I explained my predicament, and said that he would be glad to guide me to a road that would lead me to Montego Bay, if I would kindly wait until he tied up his cow. He tethered the animal to one of the stalks of bamboo, which was as large around as a pine sapling, and climbed into the car with me. His name, he said, was Denver McCurdy. He told me that he owned a small plot of land on which he grew a few cassavas, a few yams, and a few bunches of bananas, and that he was too poor to be married. His cow's name was Annie. He said that he and Annie had been out for a walk. "She's company, sir."

We drove a few miles through the bamboo, turned off at a crossroad hardly any better than the path we had been following, and after five or six miles came to another road which, though unpaved, was the best thoroughfare I had seen for hours. Denver McCurdy gave me the necessary directions. "It's too bad I'm not neat, sir," he said. "If I was neat, I would guide you all the way to Montego Bay." The fact that he had been taken at least eight miles out of his way seemed not to occur to him. I offered to drive him back to his cow, saying that I was sure I would be able to manage now that I knew the roads, but he wouldn't hear of it—the day was almost gone, I might get lost again, and if night overtook me I wouldn't have any place to stay or anything to eat. "I'd be too fretful," he said. "You best go on to Montego Bay." He wished me a safe journey as I drove off, and when I glanced back at him the shadows were already closing in.

The braying of a jackass in the middle of the night sounds like the accumulated misery of a hundred unhappy reincarnations. And yet the ones here in Jamaica have a more agreeable life than any I know. They are never laden with the backbreaking burdens they are sometimes asked to carry in Spain, or beaten senseless as in some sandier parts of the world, and they seem to have been happily incorporated into the local kinship system. All over the island they are to be seen stretched out on the little porches of the native houses, dozing with the rest of the family. They apparently make fine pillows. By my count, one jackass can accommodate six heads, and I have rarely seen anything cozier.

Voodoo in Jamaica is called obeah: "obi" among the natives. We have here in the hotel at Tryall a tall, thin, rather ascetic-looking woman with high cheekbones and deep-set eyes, who takes care of the laundry. The other servants treat her with wary respect. They tell me that her mother was an obi-woman, as was her grandmother, and they believe she has inherited all their other-worldly powers. She never associates with them and is not often seen. Occasionally I hear her singing, however, in a muted preoccupied alto, and her song is always the same—"Rock of ages, cleft for me."

There is a firefly on this island, *Pyrophorus plagioptalmus,* that is called the "peni-walli" and is at least ten times the size of an ordinary firefly. The first time I saw one I thought that someone was going about in the darkness with a torch. I happened to be reading Monk Lewis' "Journal of a West Indian Proprietor" at the time and found this entry: "*February 18.* The rain has brought forth the fireflies and in the evening the hedges are all brilliant with their numbers. In the day they seem to be beetles of a dull reddish color, but at night they become of a shining purple. The fire proceeds from two small spots in the back part of the head. When the beetle is pressed by hand the light becomes more beautiful than any emerald, and when on the wing it seems composed of the most beautiful fire." To this, there is only one thing I would like to add—the festival of light when numbers of peni-wallies are flying about close overhead. It is as though all the constellations had left their courses, or had not yet settled into them.

The little boys who beg for pennies in Montego Bay have all taken professional names—Stonewall Jackson, Beef Bone Number One, Buck Rogers, Crocodile, and General Ike: these are some of them. Stonewall Jackson has appointed himself my protector. Yesterday, when I drove to Montego Bay for lunch, he approached me as I left my car. "Me Stonewall Jackson, sar," he said. "Me good boy me-o. This boy here, Beef Bone Number One, he bad boy. Give Stonewall Jackson a penny, sar." I told the rascal to beat it, and he smiled broadly, and when I returned to my car after lunch he and Beef Bone Number One were still there. "Bad boy come and start to let air out of tires," he said. "But Stonewall Jackson take off his belt and beat bad boy until bad boy run away. Stonewall Jackson good boy, sar, give Stonewall Jackson a penny."

He got the penny, naturally, since that kind of imagination must be rewarded, but I'm afraid it wasn't such a good idea. This morning I had to go to Montego Bay to post some letters, and even before I parked the car Stonewall Jackson came running up, with Beef Bone Number One in tow. "Good morning, sar. Stonewall Jackson watch your car, sar. Bad boy come and steal things if Stonewall Jackson don't beat um, sar." What puzzled me was where Beef Bone Number One fitted into the scheme of things— was he the bad boy Stonewall Jackson was protecting me from, taking those drubbings, or was he an apprentice, learning his trade from a master? At any rate, after I had been to the post office, I felt that he should be rewarded too, if only for thinking up his name. "Him good boy," Stonewall Jackson said enthusiastically, beaming at his associate. "*Three* bad boys come and start to steal things from car, and him help Stonewall Jackson beat bad boys with his belt until bad boys run away. Him good boy like Stonewall Jackson, sar."

When I pointed out to Stonewall Jackson that he didn't have a belt (his ragged shorts were held up by a piece of twine), he whooped with glee. "Yes, sar! That's right, sar! Stonewall Jackson beat bad boys so hard that his belt *broke*. Give Stonewall Jackson a shilling for new belt, sar." He didn't get the shilling—not yet, anyway—but the immediate future is clear. Either I must avoid Montego Bay or set aside a few extra pennies for every trip I make. I am Stonewall Jackson's pigeon. What I forgot to say is that he is nine years old.

Cudjoe—A Negro slave and runaway, deformed and ignorant, he is the closest approach to a native hero that Jamaica has produced. He enters its history around 1730, when he emerges as the leader of a band of Negro fugitives, all runaways like himself. They were called the Maroons. Their descendants are still known by that name, and there are several colonies of them on the island, numbering approximately two thousand in all. My stay in Jamaica made me curious about them, and yesterday, with my friend and neighbor C, who turned up at my hotel, I went to visit what is generally regarded as their capital city—a mountain settlement that goes by the name of Accompong.

But first the story of Cudjoe and the Maroons. When the English invaded Jamaica in 1655, most of the slaves owned by the Spaniards, who had been importing them from Africa since 1517, made good their opportunity to escape. One of their earliest historians, R. C. Dallas, in his "History of the Maroons," makes this comment: "It may be imagined that at their [the Spaniards'] departure, many of the slaves would be disinclined to follow the fortunes of their leaders, and still less disposed to submit to the conquerors. Almost every part of the island, particularly the mountains on the north and east sides of it, afforded them secure retreats."

Maroon means simply a runaway slave. The Spanish word is *cimarrón*. Hawkins in his "Voyages" uses the old English form "symaron," and while "Maroon" may have been derived from it, the likelier possibility is that it is a variant of *cimarrón*. The number of Maroons who fled to the mountains is not known. Dallas quotes an earlier commentator as placing the figure at fifteen hundred, but adds that this can be only vague conjecture. In any case, the ranks of the original fugitives were constantly increased by other runaways. They beat off all attempts to subdue or capture them and by 1730 had taken on the character of a separate, though outlaw, people. Prior to this they had no leader, or chief, and wandered about in marauding bands. But as the British pressed their attack and built a chain of forts to protect their outlying settlements, the Maroons concentrated their whole force in the mountains near the present site of Accompong and elected Cudjoe as their chief.

Though nothing is known of Cudjoe's early history, it seems not unreasonable to assume that he was a member of the Ashanti tribe. A large number of this warlike West African people were brought to Jamaica by the Spaniards, and the brother Cudjoe appointed as his second-in-command, whose name was understood by the British to be Accompong (the settlement was christened after him), was most probably given the name of Nyankonpong at birth—"Great Warrior" in the Ashanti tongue.

Our only description of Cudjoe comes down from Dallas, who, to judge from the internal evidence of his work, appears to have had access to eyewitness accounts of some of the events he related. "Cudjoe was a rather short man, uncommonly stout, with very strong African features, and a peculiar wildness in his manners. He had a very large lump of flesh upon his back, which was partly covered by the tattered remains of an old blue coat, of which the skirts and the sleeves below the elbow were missing. Round his head was tied a scanty piece of white cloth. He had on a pair of loose drawers that did not reach his knees, and a small round hat with the brim pared so close to the crown that it might have been taken for a calabash, being worn exactly to the rotundity of his head. On his right side hung a cow's horn with some powder, and a bag of slugs; on the left side he wore a machete three inches broad, in a leather sheath, suspended under his arm by a narrow flap that went round his shoulder. He had no shirt on, and his clothes, such as they were, as well as the part of his skin that was exposed, was covered with the red dirt of the Cockpits, resembling ochre."

The Cockpits—more often called the Cockpit Country—provided Cudjoe and his Maroons with an almost impenetrable refuge. One of the more isolated sections of Jamaica, it gets its name from its curious, even fantastic, topography —sharp, irregular, jagged upthrusts of limestone, hundreds of feet high in some instances, that form a bewildering maze of more or less circular arenas (hence cockpits), with steep, almost vertical walls. Better ambush country would be hard to find. It was Cudjoe's practice to dispose his command along the sides of one of these arenas, which could be entered only by a narrow defile, and await the latest force sent out by the British. Invariably it was cut to pieces. A contemporary historian, Charles Leslie, who wrote part of his "A New History of Jamaica" on the island when Cudjoe was still at large, indicated the threat posed by him and his Maroons. "They have increased to such a degree as many times to make the island tremble, and employ its utmost force against them. The severest laws have been enacted against them, the greatest rewards offered to him that kills any of them, and the choicest bodies of men have been sent against them, who have mostly been unsuccessful, and returned with more loss on their own side, than to that of the runaways. Since they first began to be formidable, the island has been at several millions of expenses, and may be at as much more before they will be reduced, if the Government doesn't alter the method of attacking them." (An interesting development: so many British details were ambushed, and so many losses inflicted, that the Cockpit Country began to be designated on maps of Jamaica as "The District of Look Behind," a usage employed by cartographers ever since.)

In 1738 a new governor came out to Jamaica, Edward Trelawny. For six weeks he continued the war against the Maroons. But then, more realistic than his predecessors, he sent emissaries to Cudjoe to arrange a truce. On March 1, 1738, he and Cudjoe met under a large ceiba, or cotton tree, in the Cockpit Country, and agreed to a peace treaty. *In the name of God, amen. Whereas Captain Cudjoe, Captain Accompong, Captain Johnny, Captain Cuffee, Captain Quaco, and several other Negroes, their dependents and inherents, have been in a state of hostility, for several years past, against our sovereign lord the King, and the inhabitants of this island . . .*

Under the terms of the treaty, it was agreed among other things that the Maroons were to live "forever after in a perfect state of freedom and liberty"; that certain tax-free lands would be theirs "to enjoy and possess for themselves and their posterity forever"; and that they were to be ruled by their own chiefs or headmen, who were to have "full power to inflict any punishment they think proper for crimes committed by their men among themselves, death only excepted." After more than two hundred years, this treaty is still in effect. By its terms the Maroons became the first, as they are now the oldest, self-governing people within the British Empire.

On the day that C and I made our visit to Accompong, we set out from Tryall, in the car I had rented, at seven o'clock in the morning. As best we could tell from the map, we had somewhere between thirty-five and forty miles to travel, across some of the least frequented roads in Jamaica. Until only a few weeks ago the last ten miles of the lap, beginning at the backwoods hamlet called Retirement, had to be managed by donkey, and it wasn't until we began making arrangements to hire a pair of donkeys that we learned the whole trip was possible by car.

On the advice of some knowledgeable Jamaica residents, I had written to Accompong in advance. I addressed my letter to "The Colonel of Maroons," which I was told was the present title of the Maroon chief, and since I didn't know how much time to allow for a reply, or if I would be in that part of Jamaica long enough to get one, I simply said that I would like to make a visit, and set the day and approximate hour I hoped to arrive. As I was taking care of these and a few other details, I couldn't help noticing that some of the people I talked with didn't think too much of my proposed excursion. I discovered that the Maroons have a dark, somber reputation all over Jamaica, especially among the natives. Their former ferocity is still remembered, and it is believed that obeah flourishes more abundantly among them than anyplace else on the island. I even heard rumors of a ritual killing in their neighborhood a few years back, and though the rumor is totally unfounded, as I was told by the police officer in charge of the district, it refuses to be put down.

By ten o'clock C and I were well into the interior, which was as forbidding and inhospitable as I had been led to believe (even with the weapons used in jungle fighting during the Second World War, an attacking force would find it hard going), and on toward ten-thirty we reached Retirement—a few ramshackle wooden houses, a dilapidated church, and a few large trees. A faded sign on one of the houses said POISON SOLD, and an old man in a slouch, wide-brimmed hat stood beneath one of the trees, minding a hog. We pulled up beside him and asked the way to the Accompong road. He gave us the directions and then added that no automobile had gone over the road as yet. "You'll be the first," he said in a thoughtful, meditative tone. "Yes, sir, the very first." This didn't seem very important to C or me, one way or the other, but eventually we began to understand the old man's interest. The road wasn't a bad one, despite the several inches of loose, shifting gravel with which it was surfaced and which caused the rear wheels of the car to sway from side to side, but there was one stretch of a little over two miles that I can't pretend I enjoyed—hewn from the face of a cliff, it was no more than a narrow shelf on which two donkeys, if they had wanted to pass each other, would have been forced to hold their breaths. The blank wall of the cliff rose on one side, and an unbroken drop of five hundred feet fell away on the other. I don't believe that that old man minding his hog truly expected us to be killed, but I wouldn't be surprised if the thought hadn't just happened to cross his mind in a speculative, dispassionate way.

We made it without any trouble, however, and after we put the shelf and the cliff behind us, the road, comfortably, began to take on a more routine appearance. It was then close to noon. We talked over the matter of lunch, which we had brought with us, and then, as we rounded a curve, we saw a boy up ahead running in our direction and waving a white handkerchief. I stopped the car to see what he wanted. He was dressed in a pair of khaki shorts, worn but clean, and a blue gingham shirt. The soles of his bare feet had been toughened to the thickness of leather. I had a hard time understanding what he said, since he spoke in the Jamaican dialect that is almost impossible for an outsider to follow, but eventually I gathered that he had been sent by the Colonel to guide us the rest of the way to Accompong. It struck me as a kind thing for the Colonel to do, but more than that I began to understand it was no legend that the Maroons thought of themselves as a separate, independent people—it was as though we had crossed the border of a distant, sealed-off country and had been greeted, in the person of the boy, by an emissary of the ruling house.

C and I decided that this was as good a place as any for our lunch. We invited the boy into the car, and after he settled himself on the back seat I asked him his name. He said it was Elias Chambers. I took him to be about sixteen years old. Though his skin was extremely dark, his features were more Aryan than Negroid. I remembered that a small band of rather mysterious people who called themselves "Madagascars" had pitched in their lot with the Maroons, and wondered if the boy might be a descendant of one of these. I put the question, only to have him look baffled.

Opening our boxes, C and I divided our lunch with him. Before he accepted his share, he slid from the car. Then, with movements almost too fast to follow, he whipped out the handkerchief with which he had flagged us down, covered his food with it, and darted behind a large tree that grew along the road. His concealment was complete; we didn't catch a glimpse of him until he had finished eating. Later, when I returned to Montego Bay, where I am putting this together, I inquired into his odd behavior. Obeah, I was told. Though we may have appeared well disposed toward him, he couldn't be sure; we might have meant him harm. By covering the food with his handkerchief, and then taking it behind the tree, he had guarded against our putting a spell on it—obeah recognizes the evil eye.

The last mile of the road to Accompong rises in a steep, unbroken climb. When we reached this stage of our journey, we found that a crowd of approximately two hundred young Maroons who seemed to range from six to sixteen, all boys, had lined up on both sides of the road to await the arrival of the visitors. Not wanting to disappoint anybody, I gave the car the gun. The wheels churned through the thick loose gravel, but after less than a tenth of a mile the car coughed, sputtered, and kicked out. I backed down to a moderately level place where the road began its final one-mile climb, shifted into low, and this time really took off—there was a whirlwind of gravel, a cry of encouragement from the young Maroons, and another panting collapse. There was nothing to do but shoulder the failure of the white man's technology, and get out and walk. I picked up a bottle of rum I had brought as a present to the Colonel (it seemed only right that I should take along something, and I hadn't met a Jamaican yet who was antagonistic to rum) and started hiking after Elias Chambers and C. As soon as I left the car, the young Maroons swarmed in on it. Some of them had never seen an automobile before.

Elias Chambers led the way up the road, his bare feet seemingly immune to the sharp stones I could feel through my shoes. (I don't want to sound more dressed up than I was, however; what I had on was shorts, a shirt with the sleeves rolled up, and a pair of loafers.) I felt just a little silly, toting a bottle of rum and trying to keep up with a Maroon boy who moved like a mountain goat, but it wasn't long before we came to the end of the road and the beginnings of the Accompong settlement. A small frame cottage, enclosed by a picket fence, stood just past the debouchment of the road, and Elias Chambers showed us to it. The cottage was painted white and had a wide veranda on all four sides. A short, muscular, middle-aged Negro was waiting on the veranda, standing before the front door. His eyes were set close together and his hair was shot with gray. He wore a heavy broadcloth suit, a six-button vest of the same material, a white shirt, a stiff collar, a black bow tie, and highly polished black shoes with knobby toes. He came down the path, stepped aside as Elias Chambers opened the gate for him, and held out his hand. He introduced himself as Captain Rowe. After he explained that the Colonel was expecting us and would be along presently, he invited us into the cottage and asked us to sit down.

The cottage was a clean, one-room affair that did not look as though it was used as living quarters. There was a large window hung with lace curtains on each of the four sides. A heavy round wooden table covered with an embroidered white cloth stood in the middle of the floor. There were several chairs, a corner cupboard full of china, and an old-fashioned phonograph with an immense tulip horn. I began to question Captain Rowe about the Maroons, but he turned my questions aside. He said that the Colonel would want to discuss these official matters with me ("official matters" was the phrase he used), and I had the impression that he was being extremely correct, anxious not to overstep his authority in any way.

In a few minutes a young woman appeared whom I guessed to be in her late twenties, and Captain Rowe introduced her as his daughter, Cora. She was animated and personable, wearing a white dress and a pair of white shoes, and she spoke with such a burry Scots accent that I had to ask her about it—she hadn't grown up in Scotland, by any chance, had she? Miss Rowe laughed and shook her head. She told us that when she went to the

Accompong school ("and that would be some time ago, as you can see"), the schoolmaster was a Scot, sent by the Crown. "Mr. McNabb, he was," Miss Rowe said. "He had the tuberculosis, the poor unfortunate man, which was why he came here, in the hope of getting over it. It was from him I learned the language, and so if I have a Scot manner of speaking, as you say, it was from his manner of speaking that I picked it up. But it must have been a long hot ride from Montego Bay. I'm sure you must be thirsty. May I offer you some coconut milk?"

No longer did I question that I was in a sovereign country—Captain Rowe the Chief of Protocol, Miss Rowe the Official Hostess, and the cottage the Accompong equivalent of Blair House. C and I said that we would enjoy some coconut milk, and Miss Rowe nodded to her father. He left the cottage, but I could see him through one of the windows. He took off his shoes, and then, with a briskness that surprised me, began to shinny up a tall coconut palm that grew in the side yard—all this in his suit and vest and high collar and black bow tie. He threw down a couple of coconuts, slid back to earth, and got back into his shoes. He hacked off the thick outer husks of the coconuts with a machete, punctured them, and brought them into the cottage, holding one in either hand. Miss Rowe poured off the milk into two large glasses that she brought from the cupboard, and we sat talking to her and her father until the Colonel arrived.

The Colonel was dressed in the same fashion as Captain Rowe, except that he hadn't put on a collar, and looked as though he might have just been roused from a nap. Miss Rowe introduced us and asked permission to be excused. Unable to think of anything else to do or very much to say, I gave the Colonel the bottle of rum I had brought along. He thanked me and spoke a few words in dialect to Captain Rowe. The Captain brought four tumblers from the cupboard, and Colonel Robertson, making just enough of a ceremony out of it, poured a drink all around. He then noticed, apparently for the first time, the glasses of coconut milk that C and I had put on the table when he entered the room. He suggested that we lace the coconut milk with rum. We did, and it improved the taste immeasurably.

The Colonel, whose full name was Walter James Robertson, was considerably taller than Captain Rowe and much older and thinner. Though he generally used dialect when talking with Captain Rowe, he spoke English well. He said he was glad to see us. Visitors rarely came to Accompong, and Americans almost never. Except for a lady named Miss Katherine Dunham,[3] he didn't think that there had been an American in Accompong in more than twenty years. What, specifically, could he do for us? He was plan-

[3] Miss Dunham is the dancer and choreographer. Some six years before my visit she spent a month with the Maroons—a longer stay than any other outsider—and she has recounted her experiences in "Journey to Accompong" (Holt, 1946). Despite an occasional error of fact—as when it is stated that the only Maroons in Jamaica are those in the Accompong settlement—Miss Dunham's account is the best day-to-day record of life among the Maroons that we are likely to have for some time.

ning to take us on a tour of the settlement, but was there anything we would like to know in advance?

I replied that there was—would he mind explaining how he had become the leader of the Maroons? I said I had read the peace treaty between the Maroons and the British, and that, as I recalled its terms, Cudjoe was to continue as chief until his death. When this transpired, authority was to devolve upon his younger brother, Captain Accompong, and then upon his other, and still younger, brother, Captain Johnny. After Captain Johnny's passing, Cudjoe having no more brothers, Captain Cuffee was to be chief, and, following Cuffee, Captain Quaco. But what then? How had the command been handed down since?

Colonel Robertson finished off his drink and poured himself another. He passed the bottle of rum to Captain Rowe, who freshened his glass, and the two men conversed briefly in dialect. At one point Colonel Robertson shook his head slowly, wrinkling his brow. "It's an old argument," he said abruptly, apparently under the impression that I had understood the exchange between him and Captain Rowe. "Some say it was the way you describe it, Cuffee before Quaco, and some say it was the other way round, Quaco before Cuffee. Otherwise, everything you say about the treaty captains is how it has been understood among us. Accompong came after Cudjoe. Johnny, however, never became chief. He died before Accompong, and was followed either by Cuffee or Quaco, depending on which side of the argument you want to take."

"And after that?"

The Colonel emptied his glass at a swallow and meditated on the taste of the rum. "These things happened a long time ago," he said. "As Schoolmaster McNabb used to say before he went away—have you heard about him? He had t.b. when he came here, and it got so bad he had to leave; they said he died in Kingston—Schoolmaster McNabb thought it a pity that none of the Maroons in those days could read or write. We would then be able to say to a visitor like yourself, 'Here is what was written down at the time.'" For a few moments the Colonel paused, looking thoughtful. "The way it has been understood among us is this. Just before the last of the treaty captains died—some say Cuffee and some say Quaco—it was decided by the council that the chief of the Maroons should always be a descendant of one of the treaty captains, if possible. And that is how it has been ever since. When a chief dies, the one who will follow him as chief is chosen by vote. An out-loud vote. Yes, that's right, oral. Any Maroon past the age of thirty may be elected, but generally, as I have said, he is picked from among the descendants of the treaty captains. The same thing is true of the members of the council, though being a descendant of one of the treaty captains is not so important. The members of the council are called Major, Captain, Lieutenant, and Sergeant. You know Captain Rowe, and we'll meet Major Foster. The Lieutenant and the Sergeant couldn't be here. They went to Maggoty yesterday, to sell some of our cane. I belong to the line of Quaco. Captain Rowe is descended from Johnny, and Major Foster traces his ancestry to Cuffee. The truth is that there is hardly a Maroon who in some degree is not related to the treaty captains. Would you like to walk around?"

Except for its location, I found nothing in Accompong to distinguish it from most backwoods settlements in Jamaica, unless it was that the houses seemed better built and in better repair. A narrow dirt road winds through the community, and most of the houses are set back from the road. Our first stop was the bakery. It looked like the other houses, with the addition of an open lean-to on one side and a large beehive oven at the far end of the lean-to. Major Foster, Colonel Robertson's second-in-command, turned out to be the Accompong baker. He was kneading a large mound of dough when we arrived, working at a long board table in the lean-to. He came forward, covered with flour, wiping his hands on his apron. We spent a few minutes with him and then went on to the schoolhouse—a squat, massive stone building that Colonel Robertson said was over a hundred years old. The schoolmaster was waiting for us. Colonel Robertson introduced him as Teacher Fraser. A twenty-eight-year-old Jamaican, but not a Maroon, Mr. Fraser told us that he had been educated in England at the Crown's expense and that he received his salary from the Jamaican government. He showed us through the schoolhouse, which smelled of chalk and is divided into four rooms, and said that he had around one hundred and twenty-five children in attendance. "But he doesn't have to look after them all by himself," Colonel Robertson interjected. "He has three of our young Maroon women to help him out, who are also paid by the government. All our children know how to read and write and how to do sums. We have the best school in Jamaica. Once a year an Inspector of Education comes from Kingston to visit the school, and he always says the same thing—that we have the best school in Jamaica. Except for the Inspector, we have no dealings with the government in any way. We pay no taxes, and we still hold our own courts, just as it says in the treaty. The English have been very good about abiding by the treaty."

My friend C is a publisher, and as he and Mr. Fraser fell into a conversation about textbooks, the reflection crossed my mind that these were the best-spoken, most intelligent natives I had met in rural Jamaica. They were admittedly a special sampling—the Accompong elite, if you like—but even so I can't go along with the version of the Maroons that has got into general circulation. What the obeah situation with them is, I can't say. But sullen and primitive?—no, I'm afraid not.

When we left the schoolhouse and continued our tour, Colonel Robertson gave me a few more facts and figures. He said the Accompong settlement comprised 4353 acres and that it was the home of approximately 650 Maroons. Among them they owned 120 head of cattle and about 250 goats and pigs. Their crops were yams, ginger, tobacco, coffee, bananas, and sugar cane. Up until a few years ago the chief money-maker was bananas. But then a blight hit the trees, ruining most of them, and now the main crop was sugar cane; Colonel Robertson said the new road would be of great help in getting the cane to market; up to now it had had to be carried out by donkeys.

The system of land tenure in Accompong is a loose mixture of private property and communal ownership. Though each Maroon family owns its own piece of land, which may be inherited, a substantial portion of the acreage—Colonel Robertson didn't know exactly how much: upward of a thousand acres, he thought—was held in common. When young Maroons marry and set up their own establishments, this reserve is drawn upon and parceled out. "We're not rich," Colonel Robertson said, "but we try to look after everybody."

C and I stayed in Accompong until almost sunset. Neither of us wanted to contend with that shelf along the cliff in the dark. Colonel Robertson and Captain Rowe walked with us to the head of the road, where Elias Chambers was waiting to conduct us back to our car. We shook hands all around, and after I thanked Colonel Robertson for his hospitality and he thanked me again for the rum, I asked if there was anything I could send him from the United States—something he would especially like to have. He hesitated a moment and then brought himself to speak. More than anything else he would appreciate a pair of American shoes. Size eight. Leather ones with rubber soles. (*Colonel Robertson wrote me a month or so later, after I had returned home. "Major Foster, Captain Rowe, Miss Cora, Teacher Fraser, and others send greet-*

ings. Everybody who has seen the shoes thinks they are lovely, and they fit fine. [Signed] Walter J. Robertson, Colonel of Maroons, Accompong, Maggoty P.O., Jamaica, B.W.I.")

The most unseemly error of the average American tourist is to imagine that the rest of the world shares his liking for the first-name familiarity that he mistakenly equates with democracy. It might be different if ours were a truly classless society, as truly it is not, and in those countries where proper deportment and good manners are taken to imply consideration of others, the American impulse to familiarity produces more misunderstanding than it engenders good will. What has caused me to go off on this tangent is that earlier this evening, when I was dining in one of the Montego Bay hotels, I heard a gray-haired American of advanced middle age, who arrived with his wife only this afternoon, trying to get the assistant manager to call him "Frank." And what he did not understand, coming as he does from the determinedly roughhewn atmosphere of western Oklahoma, was that what he was asking was close to impossible—the assistant manager is a recently transplanted Englishman. Several times he told Frank that he couldn't, sir, not really, and I noticed the relief on his face when his exchange with Frank was interrupted by one of the English guests, who strode up to the desk and brusquely demanded his key.

I know the guest in question, and he is a vain and foolish man. I don't know Frank, but I am sure that he is a much kindlier person. And what has happened? Poor Frank's feelings are hurt. He is saying to himself that he held out the hand of friendship, only to have it slapped down, and that there hasn't been an Englishman yet who wasn't a damned boot-licking snob; he is thinking of the Men's Club back home, which meets for lunch every Tuesday—a relaxed, jovial affair where everyone is on a first-name basis and where even the richest oil millionaire in town wouldn't dream of putting on airs.

Such a tangle! If I had anything to do with the State Department, I would suggest the addition of a few lines to the pamphlet it has published for the benefit of United States citizens traveling abroad: "No offense is intended when you are addressed as sir or madam, señor or señora, monsieur or madame. These and other similar usages have been found helpful to oil the wheels of society. Don't, then, throw sand in the gears. There are certain items that do not lend themselves to export, and American familiarity is one of them. As a loyal citizen of the United States you will be expected please to mind your manners, and you are requested please to do nothing that might interfere with the rights of the citizens of other countries to mind theirs. Thus international friendship will be fostered, and the cause of world peace served."

Today was Sunday and I went to the races. They were run just outside a village a few miles down the coast from Montego Bay, where a half-mile track had been staked out in a field of about one hundred acres. The furlongs were marked off by bamboo poles, and the finish line was indicated by a thicker and higher bamboo pole, to which a strip of red cloth had been tied. When I reached the track, a crowd of approximately three hundred persons had gathered, most of whom were natives. There were no seating arrangements. You watched standing up.

Ten horses were on hand, brought from various estates in the neighborhood where, during the week, they are less excitingly employed. All were entered in at least two of the scheduled six races, and some had been named to run in all. Bamboo-and-palm-leaf stalls had been built for the horses, within a paddock enclosed by barbed wire. The paddock was the center of attention when I arrived, busy with jockeys, handlers, and grooms. These were men and boys employed on the estates from which the horses had been borrowed. One of the jockeys stood out from the rest. He wore a silk hat of red and white stripes, a bit too large for him and obviously homemade. All the others were dressed in their usual workaday clothes.

Betting was provided for. Two men stood behind a counter fashioned of a plank that rested on two sawhorses under a square of canvas stretched on four bamboo poles. One took bets and the other chalked up the odds on a small blackboard which stood on an easel-like arrangement made of three pieces of bamboo. Running alongside the betting booth were six other booths—more canvas and bamboo poles—each of which was occupied by a concessionaire: a "snowball" man, a small boy churning ice cream in an ancient hand freezer, a man making waffles, a woman selling big sticks of peppermint candy, another selling cookies, and a third who presided over a crude wheel of fortune.

The meeting turned out to be a rather rough affair. In the first race a horse bolted and ran down a man, who emerged indignant but unhurt, and in another race a young woman got her bare foot stepped on as the horses turned into the stretch—she yelled, hopped about, and then began to yell louder: her horse won. The third accident involved a little boy of five or six. He was standing on the edge of the track, and when he leaned forward to watch the oncoming horses he fell foul of a hoof and received a violent blow on the head. Except for a few die-hards who made it a habit to run after the horses from start to finish, the race was forgotten. "Dead! Stone dead!" cried an old man in a torn felt hat, his voice rising above the shouts of the crowd. "Stone dead for sure!" And for a few moments it looked as though the boy had indeed been killed. His eyes were closed, his head sagged on his neck, and there was a large, bloody welt just above his left temple. A white man picked him up and began to carry him to an automobile—then, to a delirious swelling of voices, the boy opened his eyes. "But wait!" the old man cried out. "Look like him not going dead! No, him not going dead for sure! And dead he was, man! Stone, stone dead!" The boy's benefactor drove off with him to the Montego Bay hospital (he was able to return home in a few hours), and the sport continued. I never could figure out the betting. In the second-to-last race, having been handed a hot tip, I plunged to the extent of a pound. My horse won, running away from the field, and I got back exactly a pound—not the pound I had bet plus another pound, but simply my original wager. It was explained to me by one of the bookmakers that so many people had bet on that particular horse that there could be no winnings—the way he put it, I felt lucky not to owe him money.

Sir K is one of those cultivated, uprooted Englishmen one comes across in odd corners of the world. For forty years he was a member of the British Foreign Office, stationed in such widely separated places as Persia and Chile, and during the time of the Versailles Treaty his name was much in the news. Now he is a permanent resident of a hotel in Jamaica's Ochos Rios section, where I have been spending the past few days. Sir K speaks seven languages. He used to be a frequent contributor to the *Manchester Guardian* and has published leaders in *The Times*. Twice married and once divorced, he has been a widower for twenty-six years. He is short and stocky, and those who know him well would probably say that he has put on weight. He has blue eyes, thinning blond hair that is turning gray, a heavy jaw, an elongated nose, and a raspy voice. He is full of prejudices and opinions—the errors we made after the First World War; the mistakes we are making after this last one; the character of the German people; the ambitions of the Soviet Union; Winston Churchill; Charles de Gaulle; and modern painting.

Over a brandy he told me that he has never lived in

England for more than six months at a stretch since he came down from his university, and that he hasn't been home for a visit in more than ten years. "It's that English weather," he said. "All that spartan tradition, all that organized discomfort. It's rather a perfect climate here in Jamaica, and I find the natives remarkably agreeable. As a matter of fact, I enjoy their company more than I do that of most people whose skin is the same color as mine. Moreover, I'm quite content to loaf. I have never been one of those who feel that because they are engaged in mental activity they have to go out and plant a garden. All that nonsense about the English and gardens! In my whole life I've never planted a thing. This book I'm writing? Possibly it will amuse you, but I'm trying my hand at a murder mystery laid in Persia—the Persia I knew when I was a young man. I don't know if I will be able to get it published, and I'll have to think up a pen name for myself, of course, but it has given me a great deal of pleasure. What's that? A book like the earlier one, on world affairs? My dear fellow, if I wrote such a book now, putting forth my honest views, I should be tried for high treason. We've made mistake after mistake, your country as well as mine, and that's not the sort of thing your State Department or Whitehall would like to hear, is it? No, I shall continue to amuse myself with my murder mystery. And who knows? I might get it published after all, and that would make me feel quite the equal of an Oxford don. Have you noticed how many murder mysteries are coming out of Oxford and Cambridge these days?"

Port Antonio is the prettiest place in Jamaica, to my way of thinking, and it has one of the world's most beautiful harbors, though on a miniature scale. I began to wind up my visit there, and drove back to Kingston through the Blue Mountains, over the highest road on the island. It climbs through the back country to a height of over four thousand feet, and then, at a pass called Hardwar Gap, where one comes upon the most impressive view in Jamaica, it begins to drop down to the Kingston side of the range.

Cyr Moore is a peasant proprietor who lives midway between Kingston and Hardwar Gap. I stopped to buy a few bananas from him, to piece out my lunch, and we fell into conversation. Unlike the average Jamaican, who tends to be rather small in size, Cyr is a big, strapping man who has been working the land all his life. He has a wife and six children and is forty years old. His property consists of ten acres inherited from his father, and his home is a mud-and-wattle hut of two rooms, with a lean-to attached. He raises coffee, cocoa, and a few stems of bananas. He showed me part of his cocoa crop, which he was drying on a wooden platform in the sun, and told me that though in good years he will harvest as much as fifty pounds of cocoa, this year, which wasn't good, he will have less than thirty pounds to sell. He will get around ninepence a pound for it, delivered in Kingston. Later he expects to have perhaps a hundred pounds of coffee to take to market. It sells on an average for five pounds a hundredweight. Figuring in what he gets for his bananas,

Cyr's income has never amounted to more than twenty-five dollars a year. But in the half hour I spent with him and his family I found him courteous, hospitable, wonderfully gentle with his children, and always ready to smile. I'm not so foolish as to call him a happy man, but neither did he strike me as being an unfortunate one.

My last few days in Kingston were busy, and my visit with Cyr Moore more or less slipped my mind. However, on the morning I left Jamaica by plane and caught a last glimpse of the Blue Mountains as we headed out to sea, I thought of him again—how friendly he had been, and how much kindness I had met with all over Jamaica: much less distinct now, a shadow among shadows, Denver McCurdy trudged down the road.

A few hours later I was standing with my luggage outside the Miami airport. For reasons not important enough to go into, I was obliged to spend the night in a Miami hotel. I had two suitcases, a typewriter in its case, and a large wicker basket stuffed with various odds and ends. It was almost full summer, but the Florida sun didn't feel particularly warm, and the sky seemed a rather faded-out blue. A taxi drew up and the driver leaned out. He had a cracker face and a cracker voice. He said, "Hey, Mac, want a cab? It'll cost you six-bits extra for all that stuff. Anything more than one bag is two-bits each." I agreed to pay the extra six-bits, and I knew I was home.

The Last Confederate

THE LAST CONFEDERATE

ALTHOUGH Americans as a rule do not emigrate, the small Brazilian city of Americana, which is about a hundred and twenty-five miles inland from the coffee port of Santos, stands as proof that some do, for it gets its name and most of its interest from a contingent of Southerners who, in the years following the Civil War, left the ruined Confederacy to make a new start in Brazil. Its name, however, is slightly misleading. The Southerners who pioneered that part of Brazil did not settle in Americana, which used to be known as Villa Americana, or American Town. They lived on farms hacked from the jungle for some distance around it, and Americana was simply their trading post. Today it is a completely Brazilian community—a busy industrial town of approximately six thousand inhabitants, with only its name to suggest its rather curious relation to the Lost Cause.

Having been born and raised in New Orleans, I grew up knowing, in a general way, that a number of people had left the Southern states for more tropical regions during the Reconstruction era: a connection of mine, a great-uncle on my father's side, made his way as far south as Argentina. I used to hear about him when I was a boy, since he and my grandfather kept in touch with each other, and then later, when I became more solidly interested in the history of my section, I was told that a number of Southern colonies had been attempted just above and just below the equator—some in Central America, some in Mexico, and some in Brazil. Aware that most of these had failed, I was under the impression that they all had failed. I was therefore unprepared to learn, from a book about Brazil I was reading a few weeks before I was to sail for Rio de Janeiro in the summer of 1953, that the settlement around Americana had by no means gone under. I gathered that not only had it prospered in a modest way, while retaining much of its North American coloration until the early part of the present century, but that some of the descendants of the original settlers were still living in the vicinity.

For me, however, the real harpoon was a sentence I read in another book, of a much more scholarly nature. "The Confederate Stars and Bars," it said, "sometimes appears as a decoration on Indian pottery along the Amazon." That did it. I read further on the subject and made up my mind that while I was in Brazil I would see what else I could learn about the Southern émigrés who had been responsible for this intriguing ceramic example of cultural cross-fertilization. I knew that I could not track it down completely, since a trip up the Amazon was not included in my plans, but I hoped to be lucky enough to find somebody who had been raised in one of the households that had carried the Confederate emblem to Brazil and who could tell me something about the adventure at first hand.

I was luckier than I had expected to be. A week or so after I arrived in Rio, some friends told me about a man named Robert Pyles and suggested that I get in touch with him. Born on a farm near Americana, Mr. Pyles is a direct descendant, on both sides of his family, of some of the very first Southerners who arrived in Brazil. A great-grandfather and a grandfather—Colonel William Hutchison Norris and Dr. Robert Cicero Norris, respectively—were the actual founders of the Americana colony. His other grandfather, Judson Pyles, was among the earliest group of settlers.

Like practically all the descendants of the Confederate emigrants, who have since scattered throughout Brazil, Mr. Pyles no longer lives near Americana. He makes his home in a town called Baurú. Situated in the center of the state of São Paulo, it is two hundred and sixty miles northwest of the city of São Paulo, the capital of the state and the largest industrial center in Brazil, and five hundred miles west of Rio. Mr. Pyles is in business in Baurú. He owns a plant there that makes and bottles a soft drink, the basic ingredient of which is the juice of fresh oranges. I was told in Rio that it was immensely popular and that Mr. Pyles, whose holdings also include a fleet of trucks, sends his product into the interior as far as the Bolivian frontier, about six hundred miles from Baurú, and that some of his best customers are the Indians of the Mato Grosso. Interesting though this was, I was more interested in Mr. Pyles himself. I sent word that I would like to talk to him about the Villa Americanistas, as the Confederate emigrants and their descendants are generally called, and he invited me to come out to Baurú and spend a few days with him.

Since getting to Baurú from Rio by train is rather complicated, I decided to make the trip by air. One of the curiosities of Brazil is that it never quite caught up with the railroad age and went in one jump from the wagon to the plane. Consequently, though most train travel involves a considerable amount of inconvenience, it is possible to fly almost everywhere, even into the deepest jungle. I left Rio one morning at six-fifteen, reached the city of São Paulo an hour and a half later, and was on my way to Baurú in another plane at eight twenty-five. After leaving the São Paulo airport, we crossed a range of high, eroded hills—with here and there the pink tiled roof of a dwelling looking lost and lonely in their folds—that seemed as barren and inhospitable as the harshest regions of Spain. Soon, though, the character of the landscape changed, and the color of the earth with it. The parched brown wastes gave way to planted fields, and the land took on a variety of red, pink, and purple tones. Some of the fields, plowed but not planted, were the brilliant pink of a watermelon. Others, on which crops were growing, ranged from red, through mauve, to a shade almost as dark as indigo. It looked beautiful to me—the way Brazil should look, I thought. Not until later did I learn that all this was part of a vast area that is covered most of the year with a thick, choking blanket of dust, and that it was the reddish color of the soil which, for many of the refugees from the Reconstruction South, had made it seem like home.

The plane reached Baurú in just over an hour. It is a town of around forty thousand people, set in a saucer formed by a range of hills. As the plane came down, I had a quick look at it—tiled roofs and palm trees and the steeple of a church—and then, when we hit the runway, a great cloud of dust boiled up, obscuring my view. It was like landing on the water in a flying-boat; the dust fumed against the windows like the splash of waves. The runway was simply a swath of earth that had been plowed up and then rolled. Our landing, though, was smooth enough. Had it not been for the dust, I don't think I would have known that the runway was not paved.

Mr. Pyles was waiting for me. I had not been given enough information to build up any picture of him, and so, theoretically, I should not have been open to any surprise. But I was. He came up and introduced himself—I was the only passenger to get off the plane—and I'm afraid that I looked at him incredulously for a moment. I had thought it singular that he should be in the business of bottling a soft drink, which is one of the more favored forms of commercial enterprise in the Deep South, but it had not occurred to me that I would find a third- or fourth-generation Brazilian who looked as though he had just stepped off the main street of some small town in Georgia.

I was even more taken aback when he spoke to me with a Southern accent—one of the most pronounced Southern accents I've ever heard.

"I'm glad to see you," he said, extending a hand. "Did you have a good trip?"

I said that I did, and that I appreciated his asking me to Baurú. Mr. Pyles replied that it was a pleasure to have me, and we chatted inconsequentially while we waited for my bag to be taken from the plane. I judged him to be in his middle forties. He had a thin face, with the high cheekbones and lean jaw that one associates with the Scotch-Irish who make up so much of the population of the middle regions of the South, and light gray eyes. His brows and lashes were of a sandy color, as was his flat, carefully trimmed mustache. He wore a yellow sports shirt, tan drill trousers, a pair of low-cut shoes, and a straw hat with a wide, curving brim.

Although it was August, which in Brazil is the equivalent of our March, the sun had a burning glare. "It's kind of hot this morning," Mr. Pyles remarked. "Up till day before yesterday, though, it was nice and cool." He squinted at the sky for a moment—a countryman's squint: a man accustomed to reading the weather—and then resumed. "This is a funny winter we've been having. Only about five weeks ago we had a big frost that just about ruined everything, one of the worst frosts in a hundred years, and now it's most warm as summer. Maybe we'll have an early spring."

Again I was struck by his accent, along with the way he

used certain colloquialisms of the South—"up till day before yesterday," for instance, and "most warm as"—and I risked commenting on it. Just then a young Negro wearing a bright green shirt arrived with my bag. Mr. Pyles spoke to him in Portuguese, and there was a fluent exchange, and it was easy to tell that my host was more at home in Portuguese than he was in English. I didn't understand what was being said, since my knowledge of Portuguese is something less than rudimentary, but one of his remarks caused the young Negro to laugh. A couple of other Negroes came up, and they and Mr. Pyles had a brisk conversation. There was some more laughter all around, genial and easy-going, and then, turning back to me, Mr. Pyles replied to my comment about his accent. His tone was that of a man who wants to explain himself carefully. "All my people came from the South," he said. "One of my grandfathers was from Georgia and the other was from Alabama. We always spoke English at home—I learned English before I learned Portuguese—and if I have any kind of accent, I reckon I just picked it up."

Mr. Pyles' car, a fairly new sedan of American make, was parked in the shade of the larger of the two wooden buildings at the Baurú airport. It had the low, rectangular lines of a milking barn and a corrugated-tin roof splotched with rust, and whatever paint its walls once had—white paint, apparently—was discolored and peeling, almost gone. A flock of buzzards were gliding high in the sky above us, making large circles, and it occurred to me that I might just as well have been somewhere in the back country of the Deep South. All the elements were present—hot sunlight, a run-down building that needed paint, dark faces and voices in the background, and a buzzard overhead. Mr. Pyles and I got into his car, and the young Negro in the green shirt waved good-by to us as we drove off. "He was married last week," Mr. Pyles said. "Some little girl got hold of him, a little country girl who's hardly ever been to town. That's what we were joking about. It's going to work out all right, though. She's a nice girl and he's one of the best young men around."

It was about a three-mile trip into town, along a dirt road strung with barbed-wire fences. Dust lay inches thick on the shoulders of the road and swirled densely behind us. In no time at all Mr. Pyles had the car going at over fifty miles an hour. I thought that in this respect, at any rate, he was a bona fide Brazilian, for I had almost been clipped several times by exuberant drivers in Rio. I found it hard, however, to think of him as truly a Brazilian and wondered what he considered himself. I wanted to ask him but decided to put it off. Instead, I asked what grew in the fields behind the fences.

"Not much," Mr. Pyles replied. "This isn't very good farming country any more. We grow a little cotton, a little cane, and a little coffee. None of it comes to much, though. The land around here is just about played out." He paused for a moment, seeming to have made himself mildly unhappy by speaking of the deterioration of the land. "Farming in Brazil isn't like it is in the States," he continued. "We have to go a long way to catch up. The truth is that it was the Americans around Villa Americana who first taught the Brazilians how to farm. I'm not saying that. It was a Brazilian who said it to me. Years back, when I was going to Mackenzie College in São Paulo—São Paulo's where I got my education, for I went there when I started grade school and stayed until I graduated from college as a civil engineer—years back, as I was saying, there was this Brazilian girl I was going with. When I met her father for the first time, he asked me if I was related to Judson Pyles. When I said that Judson was my grandfather, he told me that he had once gone to Villa Americana and spent several days with him. 'And I'll tell you this,' he said. 'It's been over fifty years since I made that visit, but the Americans knew more about farming then than most Brazilian farmers know today.'"

We had reached the outskirts of Baurú, but Mr. Pyles kept pushing the car along at a rapid pace. "You take farming implements," he said. "Up till the time the Americans came, the Brazilians didn't know how to make a good plow. That's a fact. There was a blacksmith in Villa Americana—an Italian—who used to repair the tools that the Americans brought with them. Since they couldn't get any new ones, they had to make out with what they had. Anyway, this Italian blacksmith started a little factory to make plows, modeling them after the ones he had worked on, and today it is one of the biggest industries in the country."

The rather sharp distinction that Mr. Pyles had drawn between Brazilian and American farmers, together with the satisfaction he seemed to get out of recalling the agricultural talents of the Confederate emigrants, made me feel that his sense of self-identification was weighted on the American side. I was wrong, however. When I asked him the question that had been puzzling me, he immediately replied, "Oh, I'm a Brazilian. I couldn't ever live anywhere else. I went to the States for my first visit several years ago—I was in Texas and Alabama and Georgia—and I wasn't there a month before I started to get homesick for Brazil. This is where I belong."

By now we were driving through the streets of Baurú— a clean, pleasant, sun-drenched town with rows of small houses stuccoed in various shades of pink, yellow, and blue—and Mr. Pyles slowed down. Through no fault of his, a pretty girl in a flowered dress, musing her way across an intersection, had to skitter out of our path. Mr. Pyles glanced at her and shook his head. "You better watch out, honey," he said under his breath. "You're going to get yourself hit one of these days." I thought it was a curious way for a Brazilian to talk—a Brazilian who had been homesick in Texas, Alabama, and Georgia—but I let it pass.

Mr. Pyles said that he hoped I would be comfortable at his house. "I'm a bachelor, you know," he explained. "Up till a couple of months ago I was staying at a hotel here in town. I have a couple who work for me, and they do all they can, but it's hard for a bachelor like me to keep house, even with a housekeeper. I hate it. I think you'll make out all right, though. Maybe you would have been more comfortable at the hotel—it's a nice place, clean and well run—but I thought that your staying with me would give us a better chance to talk. I just hope that you won't feel that you've come all this way for nothing, that's all."

Mr. Pyles apologized for not being able to take me to his house immediately. He said he was obliged to stop for a few minutes at his plant. On our way there, as we drove down the main street of Baurú, which looked to me pretty much like the average American main street, except that it was narrower and all the signs were in Portuguese, I asked him to tell me about the town. He said that fifty years ago it was hardly more than a village, and that it was the railroads that had caused it to grow; several lines met in Baurú, and one of them, the Northwest Railroad of Brazil, was the only line that ran through the large and all but uninhabited state of Mato Grosso, to the west. "After you leave Baurú, there isn't much," Mr. Pyles concluded. "Just the *sertão*."

"The *sertão?*"

"The wilds."

"How wild?"

Mr. Pyles thought for a moment. "That all depends," he said. "It doesn't get really wild—deep jungle—until you come to the Grosso itself. That's where that English fellow, Colonel Fawcett, disappeared. It's about six hundred miles away. The country between here and the Grosso—well, it's hard to explain. Maybe you'd like to see some of it for yourself. I have a farm on the Tieté River—not a big place, just seventy-five acres—and I was thinking that we might drive out there tomorrow. It's around a hundred miles away. Do you like to fish?"

I said I did, and Mr. Pyles seemed glad to hear it. He told me of a game fish, called the *dourado*, that is found in the Tieté River. It runs to three and four feet in length and is bright gold in color. This wasn't the best time of the year for the *dourado*, he said, but it might be worth trying our luck. He also told me that there were a few alligators in the Tieté, if I was interested in getting a shot at one, and, living in the forests along the banks, a creature called the *capivara*. "He's a kind of wild hog," Mr. Pyles said. "He lives on land, but he can swim under water. He's an ugly devil, too. Scare the gizzard out of you if you're in a boat and one of them breaks the water alongside. Weighs sixty kilos or more. But you didn't come to Baurú to hear about that, did you? We'll get around to Villa Americana in a little while. I don't have to stay long at the plant."

Mr. Pyles' intentions could not have been better, but we didn't catch up with the Confederate exiles again until late that afternoon. The hours in between were spent visiting—first at Mr. Pyles' modern spick-and-span plant, which fronts on a square at one end of Baurú, then at the hotel, where we were joined for lunch by six of Mr. Pyles' friends, and after that walking up and down the main street. Mr. Pyles seemed to know everybody, and everybody seemed to know him. We finished our rounds by having a refreshment at the soda fountain of the local five-and-ten, part of a Brazilian chain called Lojas Ameri-

canas, at which point I gave up noting the similarities between Baurú and towns below the Mason and Dixon line.
However, it did strike me as curious that, although my
host could not be said deliberately to have arranged his
life according to the general pattern of everyday existence
in the small towns of the South, he had somehow or other
managed to do it just the same.

The first thing I asked Mr. Pyles after we finally settled
ourselves in the front room of his home, a new six-room
cottage on a residential street, was how many Southerners
emigrated to Brazil. It did not surprise me when he said
that he didn't exactly know. As far as I have been able to
ascertain, the figure has never been precisely established.
On September 3, 1865—five months after Lee's surrender
at Appomattox—the New York *Herald* reported that more
than fifty thousand persons were preparing to emigrate to
the Brazilian Empire, then ruled over by Dom Pedro II.
Brazilian newspapers raised the figure to a hundred thousand families, apparently on advices received from government agents sent to the United States by Dom Pedro
to promote emigration. Both estimates were wide of the
mark, for it seems that all told no more than five thousand
men, women, and children from the Southern states found
their way to Brazil.

"The Norrises—my great-grandfather and grandfather
—came here from Alabama," Mr. Pyles said. "I don't know
much about the old Colonel, who was born in Georgia and
was a lawyer, but my grandfather, Dr. Norris, was born

in Perry County, Alabama. They both fought in the war. The Doctor was in an Alabama regiment that was part of Stonewall Jackson's corps in the Army of Northern Virginia. Would you like to see a picture of him? It's not exactly a picture, it's a photograph that was printed in a newspaper, but it's a pretty good likeness just the same."

The clipping that Mr. Pyles handed me was of a group photograph of nine Villa Americanistas in their later years —erect, stern, patriarchal. Since I knew who they were, I can't say that I would have instantly recognized them as Civil War types, but I believe I would have. They had that unmistakable look—the pronounced resemblance that one finds in so many of the faces of the period, North and South alike. Dr. Norris, Mr. Pyles' grandfather, stood in the center of the group—a tall man with white hair, a strong nose, a flat mustache, and a high forehead seamed with wrinkles. His black suit was worn with a high stiff collar and a loose cravat. "People ask why they came to Brazil," Mr. Pyles said. "It was mostly the Reconstruction, I reckon, and the way things were in the South. I never heard much talk about it. Once they settled here, they were Brazilians. They made out all right, and they liked the Emperor, old Dom Pedro. He was always good to the Americans—a very fine fellow. But the Doctor—well, he never forgot. I reckon he *couldn't* forget. They used to tell a story in our family about how some American official, a Northern man, came to visit him at his home. That was long after the Doctor had settled in Brazil. He was getting to be an old man. At first he was so mad at the idea of having a Yankee on the place that he wouldn't see him. Finally he did, though, and he sat in his rocker while this official told him that he ought to return to the States. The Doctor didn't say anything. He just sat in his rocker looking as though he was going to cry. 'I'm not an American any longer,' he said at last. 'I'm a Brazilian. We came here, and the Emperor was good to us, and we're going to stay here. This is our country.'"

It was the Norrises' original intention, Mr. Pyles told me, to settle in a Confederate colony that was being planned in a stretch of territory, embracing nearly two thirds of a million acres, a hundred miles south of the city of São Paulo. The tract was a few miles inland and was watered by the Ribeira River. This colony, called Lizzieland, was the brain child of an ecclesiastical entrepreneur, the Reverend Ballard S. Dunn. The Reverend was the rector of a New Orleans church who had gone off to fight for the Confederacy. He named the colony after a favorite daughter. It was one of four American colonies—exclusive of the Villa Americana settlement—that were attempted in Brazil with Dom Pedro's encouragement. One of Dom Pedro's problems was finding people to populate his country; Brazil needed settlers then just as much as it needs them today. The second colony was three hundred miles north of Rio, in the state of Espírito Santo, and the third was not far from Lizzieland, on a tributary of the Ribeira River. The fourth was in a part of the country that even today is a difficult place to get to. It was in the deep equatorial jungle near the small town of Santarém, six hundred miles up the Amazon, and it was there, apparently, that the Stars and Bars were introduced into the culture of the Indians. No traces of any of the four colonies are left.

With the exception of Lizzieland, these colonies were the result of group effort. After the Civil War, emigrant associations were formed in several of the Southern states. Money was raised to send agents to Brazil to look over the country and pick out advantageous places for settlement. Once a site was decided upon, the agents, acting for the associations, drew up contracts with the Brazilian government. Provisional title to the tract was taken, with a guarantee of permanent title as soon as each emigrant paid for his holdings, which the associations would set aside in their names. The price of the land ran from twenty-two to forty cents an acre. Lizzieland, on the other hand, appears to have been a strictly one-man enterprise, and how the Reverend Mr. Dunn financed the deal is a mystery that scholarship has not yet bothered to unravel. He arrived in Rio a few months after Appomattox, was taken by the government on a tour of the more accessible parts of the country, and selected the site for Lizzieland. Then he returned to the States, where he toured the South, trying to round up settlers. Part of his promotion campaign was a book he wrote that thundered the virtues of Lizzieland. He called it "Brazil, the Home for Southerners."

The two Norrises seem to have heard of the Reverend Mr. Dunn's venture. In any event, father and son arrived in Brazil in either November or December of 1865 and visited the Lizzieland site. "But it didn't look good to them," Mr. Pyles told me. "It's some of the worst country in that part of Brazil, as a matter of fact. I reckon they were disappointed, having come all that way, but they decided to look around for some better land. The way I heard it, they bought an oxcart in São Paulo and loaded everything they had on it. You can bet it wasn't much. They must have learned that there was some good country farther inland, because that's where they headed. The old Colonel and my grandfather started out for the interior, walking most of the time, and they kept on walking until they came to a place about six miles from where Americana is today."

I said that it must have been quite a walk, considering what the roads in Brazil were probably like then, and Mr. Pyles nodded. "The way I heard it, it took them around three weeks," he said. "Three weeks to go about a hundred miles. There were a few little farms near the place where they decided to settle, but the rest of the country was about as wild as it comes. *Onças*, our Brazilian tigers, were a real danger there in those days. The old Colonel and the Doctor seem to have liked the looks of it, though. The way I heard it, it was the red color of the soil that took their fancy. It reminded them of home. Coming from Alabama, they figured that it would be good country for cotton and corn. It was, too. They made out all right."

It was now past sunset, and the room in which we were sitting was rapidly growing dark. We could not turn on any lights, because Baurú, like the rest of Brazil, was suffering from a power shortage. From twelve-thirty in the afternoon to six-thirty in the evening there was no electricity in the town. Our conversation strayed away from the old Colonel and his son, and I asked Mr. Pyles to tell me about himself. He said that he was forty-four years old and that after graduating from college he had gone to work for an American corporation that had a number of varied interests in Brazil. "I became their general manager in São Paulo, but I never liked it much," he went on. "A few years ago I left. Truth is, I've always wanted to farm. I still want to. I bought this plant here in Baurú, since I don't like to be idle, but it's my young brother, the one you met at the plant, who runs it. With him in charge of things, there's not much for me to do. My real interest is in my farm. It's not much, like I said, but if I make out all right with the land I have, I may buy more. I want to build myself a house up there, too. I like the country, and I like to hunt and fish, and if I could have myself a real farm, doing things right and looking after the land the way it ought to be looked after—well, that would suit me fine."

Suddenly there came a faint, distant cheer. I looked out a window and saw a blink of lights in the gathering darkness down the street. There was another, closer cheer, followed by another, and soon all the lights of Baurú were burning brightly. "Now we can see," Mr. Pyles said, turning on a lamp. "And as soon as the refrigerator gets going we can have a beer. It still ought to be pretty cold from this morning. Excuse me a minute. I'll ask my housekeeper to fix us a bite to eat with it. She's kind of put out with me.

She wanted me to have you to dinner here tonight and didn't like it when I said we'd eat at the hotel. You make yourself at home. I won't be long."

Mr. Pyles started for the kitchen, switching on lights as he went, and I got up to stretch my legs. I was rather surprised at the simplicity of my host's home. I had been told in Rio that he was more than moderately well off—that he was worth in the neighborhood of half a million dollars—and yet there was an almost ascetic spareness to his quarters. The room in which we had been sitting was furnished as an office—a desk, two chairs, and a single lamp. An adjoining one was equipped as a workshop, with a brand-new lathe and machine bench, a mechanical saw, and a full array of carpenter's tools. An automatic .22 rifle stood in a corner, along with a couple of fishing rods, and one wall of the room was lined with bookshelves. I went over and looked at some of the titles—"Elements of Agriculture," "Organic Chemistry," "Chemistry of the Soil," "Plane and Solid Geometry," "Oliver Twist," "The Works of A. Conan Doyle." One shelf was filled with paperback Westerns—"Trail's End," "Texas Triggers," "The Flying U Strikes"—and part of another was piled with seed catalogues from the United States. I picked up one of the Westerns and was back in my chair, riding the range, when Mr. Pyles returned. He grinned when he saw what I was reading. "I like those things," he said. "I like Western movies, too. How about a beer?"

I followed Mr. Pyles into a room on the other side of the office from the workshop, where, spread out on a low table, were a couple of bottles of Brazilian beer (quart bottles, the size that Brazilian beer generally comes in, but the brew is much milder and lighter than beer in the States); a dish of fried *mandioca*, the root of the manioc plant, from which the poorer natives of Brazil make flour and which, when fried, tastes something like a sweet potato; and a dish containing crackers and a round, delicious native cheese called *provoli*. Mr. Pyles and I sat down on a big, comfortable couch and, as we ate and drank, got back to the old Colonel and his son.

"As I said, they liked that red color of the soil," Mr. Pyles went on. "They had some money—not much, but some, and it was in gold—and they bought some farmland. That's how the Americana settlement began. Soon as they had built a house—it wasn't much of a house at first, I reckon—and after they had cleared some of the land, most of it real jungle in those days, they sent for the rest of the family. I don't know who came. I wasn't much interested when I was young, and then later, when I became interested, all the old people were gone. It's too bad. I wish I had found out more about it when I had the chance. Anyway, the way I heard it, the rest of the family had a rough time getting here. It took them almost three months from New Orleans. They ran into one storm after another, and the ship they were on was blown all the way to the Cape Verde Islands."

Despite the limited communications system of the time, word of the red-soil country of Brazil evidently found its

way to the red-soil country of the South. Within eight
months after the Norrises had cleared their first fields,
some fifty families arrived to settle near them. They were
mostly from Alabama, Tennessee, and Texas. Other emigrants followed, including a group of Georgians, and
among them was Judson Pyles. He sailed for Brazil aboard
the brig *Derby*, and this voyage was also a stormy one.
Mr. Pyles told me something about it, and later, through
another Villa Americanista, I was fortunate enough to get
hold of a more detailed account of the *Derby's* wander-
ings, in an unpublished manuscript written by a Confederate physician, Dr. Robert Barnsley, who was one of
Judson Pyles' fellow passengers.

The *Derby* had trouble from the start. Chartered in New
Orleans, the little vessel was scheduled to sail early in
November 1866 from Galveston, where her would-be
passengers were encamped. However, because of various
complications, most of which had to do with financial
claims against the vessel, it was January of 1867 before she
even arrived in the Texas port. "Discontent and grumbling
abounded in the camp," Dr. Barnsley recorded. "The state
of the camp was like the communes of the revolution in
Paris. After a meeting, a half dozen of the oldest men were
selected to purchase provisions for the voyage. Disregard-
ing the advice of Captain Cross and the sailors among the
party, they selected old fat bacon, flour, a little hardtack,
corn bread, a few beans, a little vinegar, and two barrels
of sauerkraut. The baggage of the emigrants consisted of
a mass of boxes, grindstones, pieces of mills, old feather

beds, boxes of scrap iron, old horseshoes, chairs, and stools. In the center of the saloon was a long wooden table. Between it and the staterooms, which were nothing but boxes with shelves for human bundles, there was scarcely room for two persons to pass abreast. A row of trunks was placed under the table. Ventilation was arranged by a draft between the fore and aft hatches."

Because of these conditions, public-health officials tried to prevent the *Derby's* departure, but on January 24, she set sail from Galveston with a hundred and forty persons aboard. Not long afterward, an anonymous poet contributed the following to the Galveston *News:*

O, give me a ship with sail and with wheel,
And let me be off to happy Brazil!
Home of the sunbeam—great kingdom of heat,
With woods evergreen, and snakes forty feet!
Land of the diamond—bright nation of pearls!
With monkeys a plenty, and Portuguese girls!

O, give me a ship with sail and with wheel,
And let me be off to happy Brazil!
I yearn to feel her "perpetual spring,"
And shake by the hand Dom Pedro, her king.
Kneel at his feet—call him, "My Royal Boss!"
And receive in return, "Welcome, Old Hoss!"

By the time this appeared, the *Derby*, with sail and with wheel, had run into further difficulties. Some of the ship's water casks hadn't been filled, and three days out of Galveston the whole party was put on short rations. The commune spirit boiled up again. Captain Cross was called before a tribunal and blamed for all the ship's misfortunes. "One Texan proposed that he should be thrown overboard," Dr. Barnsley reported. "The Captain tearfully asked how the ship would be managed in that case, to which the commune replied that among its members there were some competent to manage." Captain Cross was nevertheless permitted to keep his command, and the *Derby* continued on her course toward Cuba, the first lap of the voyage. This side of Havana, a big blow, unusual for that time of year, came up, and before it was over, the *Derby* was a useless wreck, high and dry on the Cuban coast. No lives were lost. "Shortly after the wreck," Dr. Barnsley wrote, "while the baggage was strewn in every direction, the party of emigrants were visited at night by thieves, one of whom was killed by the shot of a Texan. Trouble almost came of this."

Eventually the emigrants made their way overland to Havana. They stayed there for several weeks, and then, after the Portuguese consul in Havana had provided money to those who needed it, embarked on a steamship bound for New York. Upon arriving here, they were sheltered in a large building at the foot of Canal Street. "Although sectional feeling had hardly subsided since the war, many attentions were given by the benevolent," Dr. Barnsley noted. "Smallpox broke out among the colonists, but a prompt removal of the infected and vaccination of the whole party saved any further troubles."

On April 22 the party started for Brazil a second time, aboard the steamer *North American,* which was under the command of a Captain Tinklepaugh. Passage money was advanced by the Brazilian government as a four-year loan. Dom Pedro was among the first to call upon the badgered emigrants when they finally reached Rio. Pleased by his courteous manners, they were even more pleased by the good news he had to offer. He told them that they could bring in all their belongings duty free and that the money advanced for their passage from New York to Rio would be put on the royal cuff. He couldn't have made a more lasting investment in good will. Villa Americanistas still speak affectionately of Dom Pedro. It is he, rather than Washington, Jefferson, Lee, or Stonewall Jackson, who is their national hero. One Villa Americanista lady, who recently died in her nineties, and who, as a little girl, was among the emigrants aboard the *Derby,* was distinguished throughout her life as the first American to kneel to Dom Pedro when he came to pay his courtesy call in Rio.

So much for the trials of the travelers. At its peak, between 1880 and 1895, the settlement near Villa Americana numbered approximately thirty-five hundred people, or five hundred families. Most of the adults in these families had moved there directly from the States. The rest were refugees from the Lizzieland, Santarém, Espírito Santo, and Ribeira colonies, all of which had failed or were about to. Practically the whole of the Confederacy was represented in the countryside around Villa Americana—Alabama, Georgia, Louisiana, Mississippi, North Carolina, South Carolina, Tennessee, and Texas. (Only Arkansas, Florida, and Virginia were missing. The Arkansans and Floridians seem to have stayed at home, and the Virginians struck out in a different direction. Under the leadership of Matthew Fontaine Maury, the great oceanographer, they went to Mexico. It was not a happy enterprise, however, and the attempt to establish a colony was soon abandoned. A similar effort in Central America also came to an early end.) The majority of the Confederate émigrés to Villa Americana raised Brazil-size families, some of them running to as many as fifteen children. Both of Mr. Pyles' grandfathers, Dr. Norris and Judson Pyles, had ten—five boys and five girls apiece. "When my Grandfather Norris died, I had fifty-three first cousins on his side of the family alone," Mr. Pyles said.

The early Villa Americanistas kept as close as they could to the way of life they had known in the United States. They married principally among themselves, adhered to their various forms of Protestantism, and spoke more English than Portuguese. For the most part, they built wooden houses ("Southern-style," Mr. Pyles called them) instead of the stucco-and-tile ones Brazilians favor, but none of these approached the size and splendor of plantation mansions. Compared to the vast principalities of the plantation South, their properties were small, being numbered in the hundreds rather than the thousands of acres. Nearly all their houses are gone now, and there are few of their holdings that have not passed into other hands.

At first the chief crop was cotton, but in a short time this gave way to the large-scale cultivation of watermelons. The Brazilians had melons of their own but not water-melons, and these soon outdistanced the native varieties in popularity. After the railroad pushed its way to Villa Americana from São Paulo in the early 1890's, from fifty to a hundred carloads were shipped to market daily. The introduction of the watermelon to Brazil is generally credited to a Georgian named Joseph Whitaker, who is said to have brought the first seeds with him from his na-tive state. Even today the watermelons of Brazil have, in their own expatriate way, a Georgia look.

According to Mr. Pyles, the Villa Americana colony be-gan to break up around 1900. By then the first native-born generation had come of age. Life in Rio and São Paulo seemed more alluring to many of them than life on the farm, and the drift to the cities began. Some of the chil-dren of the original settlers, influenced by the tales they had heard of the lost homeland above the equator, went to the United States. These, however, were relatively few— Mr. Pyles thought not more than fifty. Others settled in small communities in the interior of Brazil, some to marry into Brazilian families and, in all but their Anglo-Saxon names, to become completely Brazilian. But the great majority established themselves in the cosmopolitan cen-ters of Rio and São Paulo. They became doctors, engineers, lawyers, surgeons, dentists, and schoolteachers. Most of their male descendants—Villa Americanistas of the second native-born generation—have followed the same professions. Nearly all speak fluent English, generally with a Southern accent.

Throughout my conversations with Mr. Pyles, I thought I could guess why the refugees from Reconstruction had selected Brazil as their new homeland, but finally I put the question directly—why had they? It did not surprise me too much when Mr. Pyles said that one of the reasons was that slavery was still an institution in Brazil at the time. The slave trade was banned in 1853, but slavery itself was not abolished until 1888. "That, though, was only *one* reason," Mr. Pyles emphasized. "The way I heard it, the big reason they came to Brazil was that they knew they would be welcome here. Old Dom Pedro was anxious to build up his country. He had agents promoting immigration all over the South. The main office was in New Orleans. So far as slavery was concerned, there wasn't much of it around Villa Americana. Practically none. Only two or three of the settlers ever became slaveholders. Generally they did what my people did. They worked the land themselves. When they needed labor they paid for it."

Around 1920, when Mr. Pyles was a boy, the Villa Americana colony had shrunk to its 1867 proportions; only fifty families remained. "Practically everybody lived on the land," he told me. "We had American-style buggies to run around in—there were no buggies like that in Brazil before the Americans came—and we did a lot of visiting back and forth. We used to have dances in the barns. The music would be a guitar, an accordion, and sometimes a

violin. We danced Brazilian dances mostly—our favorite
was the maxixe, which is something like the samba—but
we also danced polkas and mazurkas. At Christmas, four
or five families would get together. We'd cut a big tree and
decorate it. It wasn't anything like the Christmas trees you
have in the States, but since so few of us knew the difference, we never thought of it. We'd have Santa Claus, too,
and a great big Christmas dinner. A big dinner, though,
wasn't specially unusual. All our dinners were big. We'd
have two or three vegetables, two or three kinds of pork—
bacon, pork chops, and roast—and all the milk we could
drink. There would be whole milk, separated milk, and
buttermilk on the table at every meal. Sometimes there
would be game and fish, and we had biscuits and corn
bread every day. I never heard much talk about the South.
Every once in a while one of the old people would start
telling how it was back in Georgia or Alabama, but that
wasn't often. For one thing, most of the old people were
dead. The rest of us knew that our families had started in
the South, but I don't think we paid much mind to it one
way or the other. We had become Brazilians, and that's
how we thought of ourselves. This was our country and this
was where we felt we belonged."

By now it was time to go out to dinner. Mr. Pyles and
I promised ourselves that we would resume our conversation later that evening, but once again, with no great resistance on our part, we got caught up in a round of visiting. In fact, what with one thing and another, I didn't get

back on the trail of the Confederate settlers until several
days later. Early in the morning, a bit groggy after all our
visiting, we got into Mr. Pyles' car and left for his farm.
Ten or fifteen miles outside Baurú we came to the beginnings of what Mr. Pyles had called the *sertão*. Some of the
land has been cleared for *fazendas,* or coffee plantations,
but most of it is a scrub-country wilderness. The road got
worse and worse as we drove into the interior, and the
landscape emptier and emptier. The houses stood miles
apart. Most were of mud and wattle, thatched with palm
leaves. Rising from the little yard in front of each house, or
else nailed to one of the beams of the roof, was a tall, slender pole to which was attached a wooden frame holding a
picture of one of the saints, printed in black on a square
of white cloth about three times the size of a handkerchief.
St. Joseph and the Virgin were the favorites. Now and
then we met a horseman mounted on one of those small
ponies that are common in Latin-American countries, and
once, as we came to a stretch of fairly open hilly country,
we passed a herd of cattle attended by a pair of gauchos
riding mules.

But the most striking aspect of the countryside was the
dust. It covered everything. The trees and bushes, the
fence posts, the houses, the pictures of the saints—they all
looked as if they had been caught in a downpour of crim-
son rain, thick as paint. The dust lay on either side of the
road like drifts of sand, dune-high in places. There was
only a narrow strip of road, comparatively level but full
of ancient ruts and potholes, for the car to pass along. We

pitched and lurched, stirring up the dust. There was no escaping it. Even when we closed the windows, and baked, it sifted up through the bottom of the car. It settled on our faces, got between our teeth, and powdered our hair.

Mr. Pyles' farm lies on the south bank of the Tieté River not far from where that stream empties into the Paraná, which, in turn, flows into the Rio de la Plata. After we had cleaned some of the dust off us, we took a walk around part of the property. The farm is worked by a Brazilian farmer and his two sons. They and the rest of the family live in a five-room house, which used to be occupied by the farm's previous owner. Before Mr. Pyles bought the property, they lived in a wooden shed. It is still standing, and I noticed an inscription painted over the door: *Deus Proteja Esta Casa.* Noon had come, and the sun was high and hot. A small parrot with a yellow head croaked in one of the trees, hanging upside down. Mr. Pyles said how about our trying to catch ourselves a *dourado*, and I couldn't think of a better idea. We returned to the house, put an outboard motor in the back of the car, and drove down a weedy lane that led to the river, where we found a long, narrow skiff pulled up on the bank. I took it to be about fifteen feet stem to stern and not more than three feet wide amidships. It looked not unlike one of those primitive craft that are hollowed out from a single log. We attached the outboard, stowed away our gear and a lunch we had brought along, and started fishing. Mr. Pyles ran the outboard while I trolled. I trolled the rest of the morning and the better part of the afternoon, but I didn't get a strike. There were mudbanks in the river where the alligators sometimes lie in the sun, but we did not see any. We did not see any *capivaras,* either. Mr. Pyles thought that the noise of the outboard might have frightened them away.

I was annoyed at my bad luck, knowing that I would not soon get another chance to catch a *dourado,* but I liked being on the river. We cut off the outboard and started paddling. Without the motor going, the only sound was the flow of the river. It was wider than I had anticipated—over a quarter of a mile—and the woods along the banks, while thick, were not nearly as dense and matted as I had imagined they would be. The skiff handled well. A huge flock of ducks took flight as we rounded a bend—hundreds; exploding all at once—and all along the riverbank herons and egrets roosted in the trees. Drifting close to shore, I saw a clump of yellow orchids in the woods. Wanting a closer look, I headed the skiff into the bank. As I stepped ashore, I remembered to ask Mr. Pyles about poisonous snakes— were they many? "Just about all our snakes are poisonous," he said offhandedly. "But I haven't seen a boa-constrictor around here in some time."

Late in the afternoon we decided to call it a day. But before we left for Baurú we took another walk around the farm. Spring planting had begun, and some of the crops were already up. Mr. Pyles showed me his corn, potatoes, strawberries, and watermelons. On another part of his farm we looked at his coffee and castor beans. He had just acquired a brand-new American tractor and was putting in a complete irrigation system. As we were walking through a field of young coffee bushes, he reached down and scooped up a handful of earth. "This is good soil," he said, crumbling it and letting it fall through his fingers. "Give it a chance and it will grow almost anything. All you have to do is to help it out." He brushed off his hands and looked about him. "We were hurt by that frost—it ruined nearly all our coffee and castor—but that kind of weather is unusual. You could have yourself a real farm up here. It could be a good life for a man."

We returned to Baurú that evening. I spent the following day there, and early next morning set out on a five-hour, roundabout journey to Americana. It was just before noon when I arrived. I walked from one end of the town to the other, looking for possible signs of its Confederate origins, but I couldn't find any. Americana seemed to me to be a more prosperous and newer-looking Baurú. It has an unusually attractive *praça*, in which all kinds of colorful tropical plants have been tamed into the strict designs that adorn a formal garden, and a spanking new hotel. The whole place looked rather Italian to me, especially the *praça,* and when I went into the hotel for lunch and fell into conversation with the manager, who spoke French, I learned that at least a third of the people in Americana have an Italian background. "The Villa Americanistas and the Italians came to Brazil about the same time, and they always got along well together," the manager told me. "I know of at least one instance where an Americanista married an Italian girl. They had four daughters, true beauties, all of whom married and moved away. So have most of the other Americanistas. One could say that Villa Americana has now become Villa Italiana. Brazil is a melting pot, too."

After lunch, in the harsh light of midafternoon, I hired a car to drive me to the old American cemetery a few miles outside the town. It is a walled plot of land about the size of a city block. Within the enclosure stands a small brick chapel in good repair, before which rises a double row of high, slender palms, and in the cemetery itself there are other palms, rustling above the graves. No one else was in the cemetery, and it looked as though it was not often visited. I walked around in the hot, still sunlight, reading the inscriptions—McKnights and Burtons and Radcliffs and Thatchers and Whitakers—and came finally to the headstones of Mr. Pyles' ancestors. One read, "In Memory of Col. Wm. H. Norris. Born in Oglethorpe County, Ga., U.S.A., Sept. 17th, 1800, and Died July 13, 1893. Age 93 Years." The worn letters on the headstone of his son, Mr. Pyles' grandfather, spelled out a simpler legend: "Dr. Robert Norris, a Confederate Veteran, 7-3-1837—5-14-1913."

Cemeteries are lonely places, and I had the usual lonely feelings—Oglethorpe County and the Confederacy seemed so very far away. But even so I think that in the silence, had I wanted to, I could have heard the distant sound of drums. I remembered Mr. Pyles, standing in his fields and brushing the earth from his hands, ready to continue the Confederate adventure, and I thought that they would have understood one another—he and the old Colonel and the old Colonel's son.

South Seas Diary

SOUTH SEAS DIARY

MUCH as I like long sea voyages and freighters, I'm afraid that this time I'm outward bound on a lemon. For present purposes, I'll call her the *Island Cloud*. Beyond that, it is enough to say that I boarded her somewhere west of Suez, that her running time to Tahiti from the port where I embarked is nearly three weeks, that she carries eleven other passengers and a mixed cargo, and that she must be one of the scurviest ships afloat—slack, dirty, eaten away by rust, full of cockroaches, and, in the vocabulary of the gourmets of the merchant marine, a bad feeder.

When I came aboard a fortnight ago, half a cherry pie was lying squashed in one of the scuppers. It is still there. The decks have been hosed down exactly once, and if it weren't for a few big rains we've had, we would be knee-deep in soot. Even so, that piece of pie has turned coal-black, and it seems to me that some of the cockroaches who share my cabin are looking a little grimy. They also seem to be looking a little undernourished. The whole ship's company is having a hard time getting a decent meal. On a voyage as long as this, food assumes more than nutritional importance. Meals are the only social events of the day. Most of our sociability, however, takes the form of grumbling. Each morning we get a mimeographed menu listing the choices for breakfast, lunch, and dinner, in a sort of forlorn imitation of the stylish transatlantic liners, and invariably there are a number of stylish transatlantic dishes offered, some even in French. All would be well if we could eat the menus. The food itself is unbelievably bad, and there isn't a man among my tablemates who hasn't lost weight. One of them, a gray-haired, kindly grandfather in his early sixties, who is an engineer member of the crew, is down twelve pounds. During the war he had a ship shot out from under him and was adrift in an open boat for nine days. Hallucinations set in before he was rescued, and he was brutally burned by the sun. Lately, however, he has begun to sound as if the *Cloud* were the worst experience.

We don't fly the colors of the Royal Yacht Club, and there are those among us, especially in the deck gang, who might have been recruited from one of the old Australian prison hulks. The chief steward is a short, stout Chinese who goes around in straw slippers, a dirty undershirt, and a pair of khaki trousers, and has a set of buckteeth that give him the appearance of wearing a perpetual grin. A great deal of our ill temper is sent in his direction, and if there is another disaster like tonight's dinner, he is likely to be fed to the sharks. According to the first mate, however, our Oriental friend can't be held responsible for the melancholy quality of our diet. The owners of the freighter operate a couple of luxury liners, and, the way the mate tells it, when the food in the lockers of these vessels no longer qualifies for luxury consumption it is transferred to the lockers of the *Cloud*. The ice cream we get would seem to bear this out. It looks like real classy stuff, with three different tiers and flavors; its only drawback is that it has the flat, grainy tastelessness of ice cream that has melted and been refrozen several times over. Except as an irritant, the ice cream doesn't matter. Coffee that might have been brewed from last year's acorns is an entirely different proposition.

The truth is that the *Cloud* is a sour ship all the way through. The captain could hardly be less respected—an aging Scandinavian, he seems to think he is the only mariner ever to have gone to sea as a boy, and in his jollier moments he refers to rum as "mother's milk," God help us! And there isn't one of his men who wouldn't rather be on a shorter, less monotonous run. It will be five months before the *Cloud* completes her round-trip voyage, and tempers, strait-jacketed by confinement, are already wearing thin. We have a couple of feuds burning between decks, and some of the officers speak to each other only when they have to, and then just barely.

Today's diversion is that the plumbing went on the fritz. It is one of the characteristics of the *Cloud* that things are always breaking down. Even her engines did, shortly after she left port. For fourteen hours she was a dead ship, out of commission. The engineers finally got her going again, and since they have been looking less tense lately, I guess we'll make it. At first I had the notion that I might like to ride the *Cloud* to the end of her voyage, but I've changed my mind. My own kind of cabin fever has set in, and for reading material I'm down to "Sailing Directions for the Pacific Islands," Volume III (United States Hydrographic Office, Washington, 1952).

Playing the record back now that I am ashore, I find that the only gripe I'd want to erase is the one about reading material. "Sailing Directions" kept me entertained for hours. It is not a book I would recommend to any man over forty, since by virtue of the very names of the places it describes—Aitutaki and Raratonga and Tahaa, and so on—it becomes a sort of Bowditch's "Practical Navigator of Escape." Though I read every line at least once, and expect to live to regret it, what most held my attention was the volume's description of Tahiti, where I shall be for a month. It interested me to learn that Tahiti, as the largest of the Society Islands (17°38′ S., 149°25′ W., H.O. Chart 2065), is thirty-three miles long, northwest to southeast, and about fifteen and a half miles wide, and is formed by two ranges of mountainous land rising to considerable heights from a low and generally narrow margin of coast, and connected by the low, narrow Isthmus of Taravao. "Of these two parts," the book goes on, "the northwestern and larger is named Tahiti, and the southeastern, Taiarapu Peninsula. Mount Orohena, the highest mountain, is 7,339 feet in height, and on Taiarapu the highest is Mount Roniu, which reaches a height of 4,341 feet. A barrier reef surrounds the island at a distance of one to two miles. Within this reef there are several good harbors, the principal being that of Papeete, on the northwestern side, and Port Phaeton, on the southwest side of the Isthmus of Taravao."

After a day ashore, I am knowledgeable enough to amend "Sailing Directions" to the extent of adding that Port Phaeton is rarely used nowadays, and never by any of the larger ships. Papeete is the port of call. Because of Tahiti's barrier reef and the shoals on either side of the entrance to its harbor, the passage is best negotiated during the daylight hours (after six in the morning and before six in the afternoon), under the guidance of a local pilot.

We sighted the island just after dawn this morning, my nineteenth at sea. Fittingly enough, my last night aboard the *Cloud*—now on her way to more distant places—was particularly disagreeable. We had slowed down to around nine knots, there was hardly a breath of air, and my filing-case cabin was so stifling that I slept, as best I could, on deck. Except for the soot, I didn't mind. What had laid me low was Captain Mothersmilk (I thought that after forty years at sea he should have picked up at least *two* salty sayings), the increasing impudence of the cockroaches, and the fact that if it had not been for that cunning contraption, the egg, I would have been living mostly on bread and water. Though the larger part of my sympathy had always been on the side of Captain Bligh, minute by minute I could feel myself nudging closer to Mr. Christian.

But when morning came, and Tahiti rose in the distance out of the mist, and then the nearby island of Mooréa, I felt that the whole long trip was worth it. Air travel has its points, if you don't mind being sealed like a sales slip in a pneumatic tube, but I don't see how it can be argued that any country not totally landlocked should be approached except by sea. I will agree with those who say that one's first view of Tahiti is not as beautiful as that of the harbor of Rio de Janeiro, which I was once lucky enough to approach under similar circumstances—at dawn, after many days at sea—but it struck me as infinitely more endearing. Beyond Rio lies the vast subcontinent of Brazil. Tahiti rises from the sea whole and complete—the sharp upthrust of its mountains, the greener luxuriance of its shoreline, and the ceaseless foam of the surf breaking over the barrier reef. It was easy to understand why the island shone brighter than paradise in the forecastles of the whalers and clipper ships, and I began to forgive the *Cloud.* She had got me there at exactly the right moment, sloppy old tramp though she was, and while I will never remember her fondly, I shall always be in her debt.

Friends were waiting for me on the dock, with leis. These were made of a small white flower called *tiare Tahiti,* a true gardenia, and already I have come to think of their fragrance as the dominant odor of the island. Being the only passenger to disembark, I was through immigration and customs in no time at all, and having breakfast with my friends at a table on the terrace of Papeete's one sidewalk café, facing on the main street of the town. Since my social life on the *Cloud* had been something less than exhausting, I was too busy wallowing in conviviality to do more than glance at my new surroundings: the rather untidy main street, with a line of flowering trees running the length of the waterfront; Mooréa in the distance, and the sun on its peaks; brown people on bicycles and other brown people afoot; and Papeete itself a somewhat dilapidated, run-down town of wooden buildings and rusty tin roofs, the whole permeated with the acrid smell of copra rising from the docks. A huge, shapeless woman in a Mother Hubbard rode past on one of the bicycles, an extremely pretty girl in a yellow skirt and halter sped by on another, and an old, decrepit hulk of a man, bloated and gross and dirty, eased himself into a chair not far from us. Barefooted, he wore a pair of torn khaki shorts, the rags of a shirt, and a big straw hat. One of my friends identified him as Paul Gauguin's illegitimate son. A panhandler and renowned drunk, he had been let out of jail only the day before.

Some thirty thousand people live in Tahiti, over half of them in Papeete. The island is divided into twenty districts, roughly equivalent to counties, but in terms of local usage it falls into three parts—Papeete, the country, and the peninsula. The country is anything a couple of miles or more from Papeete, and the peninsula is the Taiarapu Peninsula of "Sailing Directions." From the center of town to the tip of the peninsula is no more than thirty miles, but the only road on the island, which circles Tahiti proper along the edge of the sea, cuts across the narrow isthmus that leads to the peninsula, skipping the latter and leaving it more or less isolated. Few outsiders go there, and its inhabitants, living primitively and clinging to a few customs that have all but vanished from the rest of Tahiti, are looked upon much as the backwoodsmen of deepest North Carolina and Tennessee are looked upon elsewhere in the United States. The peninsula is the only place where I have seen women going about bare from the waist up, and then only two very old ones. This custom was prohibited by the French administration a few decades ago, and there is now less exposure in Tahiti than on Jones Beach.

My own living arrangements are almost too civilized. I am occupying a wood-and-bamboo bungalow with a thatched roof, on the edge of a lagoon, out in the country. The bungalow is really a single large room divided by partitions to make a sitting room, a bedroom, and a bath with a shower and water closet. The habitation is one of a dozen similar ones attached to the hotel—quite a good hotel— where I take my meals.

Though I am the sole human occupant of the bungalow, I don't live alone. I share my quarters with ants, lizards, and spiders and am occasionally visited by a land crab. The spiders are large and hairy, the ants small and greedy. Having started out with a passion for chocolate mints, the ants now adore aspirin. I don't know where they live, and the land crabs are migrants from a different culture, but the spiders and lizards dwell in the thatch of my roof. All other thatched roofs in Tahiti are similarly tenanted. Without having been able to count noses in my domicile, I would say that the lizards make up the huge bulk of the population. Most of them are small green ones, friendly and companionable, but I have a few that look like teenage iguanas. These keep to themselves and croak. The noise they emit is that of a cricket trying to sound like a bull alligator. Old Tahiti hands tell me that this is the lizards' mating call. It is now their mating season, and there are evenings when the upper atmosphere of my bungalow gets quite erotic.

After the day spent circling the island in a French car I have rented, it behooves me to be careful. For once you get outside Papeete, which hasn't too much to recommend it, this place is so beautiful that it would be easy to sound like one of those maiden New England ladies mentioned by D. B. Wyndham Lewis in another connection who write books with titles that begin "The Lure of ——." Aware of the danger, I nonetheless find it impossible to be still. The truly hot days are upon us, with occasional crashing downpours, and the island is like a huge garden. The flamboyants bloom everywhere, hibiscus seems to grow wild, and up in the mountains, where I went yesterday on an all-day picnic, lantana is a pest. Under these circumstances, and with the scent of *tiare Tahiti* spreading like a stain across the darkness outside my window, it is hard not to succumb. I remember that James Morrison, one of the mutineers of the *Bounty*, was so taken with the flowers and fruits of Tahiti that he devoted a whole section of his journal to them.

Matavai Bay, where the *Bounty* was anchored for three months in 1788 while breadfruit plants were put aboard to be transported to the West Indies and the mutiny was

coming to a boil (reason: girls), is only a few miles up the
road. To this degree, Tahiti is Captain Bligh's island. It
belongs even more to that supreme English explorer Captain James Cook, who was sent here in 1769 by the British
Royal Society to observe the transit of Venus across the
sun, and certainly the two discoverers who, only a couple
of years earlier, came across Tahiti within eight months
of each other—the Englishman Samuel Wallis and the
Frenchman Louis Antoine de Bougainville—belong somewhere in the picture. Other names can be added to Tahiti's
cast of characters—those of Pierre Loti and Henry Adams,
for instance, both of whom stayed awhile on the island
and wrote about it, Loti in fiction and Adams in some of
the best of his letters—but I suppose it was Paul Gauguin
who most impressively claimed Tahiti for his own. His
myth—that of the overcivilized modern man seeking refuge
and renewal among an unspoiled primitive people—together with the reputation that Polynesians in general
have for sensuality, accounts for some of the latter-day mis-
conceptions about Tahiti. And his pictures have helped, of
course. One of the roughest renegades of the *Cloud* had
a paperback edition of Gauguin reproductions stowed
away in his gear. All he knew about the painter was that he
"took off and shacked up," and though this way of putting
it reduces the myth to its lowest possible denominator,
without trimmings, it does get to the heart of the myth, if
not of the man.

The trimmings of the myth are best found in Gauguin's
"Noa Noa," the short, impressionistic book he wrote about

his first stay in Tahiti, which lasted two years. On my tour of the island, I stopped at the place where he used to live —coconut palms, underbrush, silence, the waters of a lagoon—and this afternoon, sitting on my porch and glancing up every now and then at the clouds and shadows on Mooréa, I reread "Noa Noa." The title translates into English as "Fragrant," which was probably intended as a tribute, and the book itself is rather spotty. Too often you get a muzziness reminiscent of Sherwood Anderson and D. H. Lawrence at their worst ("Civilization is falling from me little by little . . . I am entering into truth, into nature"), and the book is slowed up by a lot of questionable anthropology, but, like so many painters (Delacroix and Van Gogh are two that come immediately to mind), Gauguin could write extremely well about some matters. His book is full of small, exact pictures that suggest the larger, more poetic ones he painted ("After she had finished drinking, she let go of the rock, caught the water in both hands, and let it run down between her breasts"), and in a few quick strokes he is able to do nicely with a landscape ("The path leads through a confusion of trees—breadfruit, ironwood, pandanus, bouraos, coconut, hibiscus, guava, giant-ferns. It is a mad vegetation, growing always wilder, more entangled, denser, until, as we ascend toward the center of the island, it has become an almost impenetrable thicket").

There isn't enough in "Noa Noa," however, to give it much value as a piece of literature. Its importance lies almost wholly in its relation to the myth that Gauguin fostered. And what has to be remembered here is that the book wasn't written until after Gauguin had left Tahiti and returned to Paris in 1893. Thus, it is a remembrance of things past, and a highly sentimental one. Gauguin lived with a thirteen-year-old girl named Tehura ("a large child, slender, strong, of wonderful proportions"), and because of what can be regarded only as the author's reluctance to inquire into the true nature and substance of their relationship, the greater part of "Noa Noa" is occupied with the story of a romance as idyllically unreal as the story of the bird-girl Rima in W. H. Hudson's "Green Mansions," and far less convincing.

It could be argued that instead of entering into truth, into nature, as Gauguin claimed he was doing, he was doing precisely the opposite. "Noa Noa" is so befogged with sentimentality that it is practically worthless as a biographical record, bearing no more resemblance to Gauguin's actual life in Tahiti than some of his more dreamlike pictures—"The White Horse," for instance, or "Contes Barbares"—bear to the actual Tahitian scene. His enthusiasm for the island lasted only a few months while he was on it; then he began falling into spells of suicidal depression, became sick, and spat up alarming quantities of blood. Presently, he had sunk into such a state that the authorities repatriated him to France. However sympathetic one may be to Gauguin, and however charmed by his pictures, it is difficult not to get impatient when he ends "Noa Noa" with this:

Farewell, hospitable land, land of delights, home of liberty and beauty!

I am leaving, older by two years, but twenty years younger; more *barbarian* than when I arrived, and yet much *wiser*.

Yes, indeed, the savages have taught many things to the man of an old civilization; these ignorant men have taught him much in the art of living and happiness.

Above all, they have taught me to know myself better; they have told me the deepest truth.

Was this thy secret, thou mysterious world? O mysterious world of all light, thou hast made a light shine within me, and I have grown in admiration of thy antique beauty, which is the immemorial youth of nature. I have become better for having understood and loved thy human soul—a flower which has ceased to bloom and whose fragrance no one henceforth will breathe.

This is a hot night, hushed with the fecund stillness that comes before the rain, but all these "thou's" and "thy's," even allowing for the translation, leave me cold. When I think of Van Gogh's cry in his autobiography—"How can I be of any use in the world? Cannot I be of any good?"—I know I am in the presence of a sincerity as sharp as pain, but in Gauguin's book the transfiguration he claims for himself strikes me as being close to phony all the way through. Any man as deeply touched with grace as he proclaims to be might be expected to live the rest of his life not necessarily without torment (did even the saints?) but with a different kind of torment. If Gauguin had really undergone such an experience, his myth might have some validity, and "Noa Noa" might be accepted on its own terms, but I don't think it can be. I see it as an almost wholly "literary" performance, raddled with bad Mallarmé, and far less honest, in every respect, than the angry, bitter journals that Gauguin kept during his second stay in the South Seas. However, I seem to be moralizing, which, now that I think of it, is an odd pastime in Tahiti. After all, Gauguin undoubtedly painted more beautiful pictures than he would have if he had never come here, and, in the end, that is all that matters.

After leaving Tahiti in 1893, Gauguin spent two years in France, maintaining himself and a young Indonesian mistress on a legacy from an uncle. He rented a studio in Paris, held an exhibition of his pictures that was more fiasco than failure, picked up syphilis, suffered a broken ankle in a brawl while on a visit to Brittany, and returned to the South Seas in 1895. Nor was it the "mysterious world of all light" that called him back. He simply remembered Tahiti as an inexpensive place to live. But again misfortune and his own temperament dogged him. Tahiti, for one reason and another, proved so irritating that he left it for good in 1901 and went to the island of Hiva Oa, in the Marquesas—a change of scene that changed nothing. He set up housekeeping with another girl in her early teens, drank prodigiously, kept up a running battle with the local officials, began taking morphine because of lingering pain in his ankle, continued painting, dreamed of returning to France and getting the recognition he knew his talent deserved, and died, one of the most abjectly miserable of men, on May 8, 1903, at the age of fifty-four.

As seen here in Tahiti, just a few miles down the road

from where Gauguin used to live, the myth that has been built up around him takes rather a beating. Nor is it made any more attractive by the presence on the streets of Papeete of Gauguin *fils*. He is the son of Tehura, and he has the most interesting pitch of any panhandler I have ever run into. Tourists with cameras are his prey. Whenever he spies one, he lumbers up as fast as he can, bows, and gets in his wedge. "Gauguin," he says. "Photograph, five francs." And I must say it works. We had a plane and a cruise boat here over the weekend, and he cleaned up.

Now it is half past one in the morning and too hot to sleep. Everything sticks, including me to my chair. I am wearing a towel and using another. The rain that has been threatening since early evening still hasn't come. Everything waits, even the lizards. The sound of the reef has died to a whisper, as it sometimes does, and when a fish jumps in the lagoon, only a few feet from my front porch, it is as if the silence itself had splashed. Now and then a coconut crashes to earth, as loud as a pistol shot, and in between there are the softer, plumper fallings of breadfruit. The smallest sounds are magnified—the whine of a mosquito, a moth batting its wings along one of the walls, a stealthy crawling in the dark. Most probably a rat, alas! Tahiti is full of them. They climb the coconut palms and spoil the fruit. Along with a few other things, they also tend to spoil the idea of Tahiti as paradise.

And now, after a few solemn warning drops, the rain comes down like the Flood. Nothing exists but its sound. One is contained in it as in a bathysphere, and no matter

how violent the downpour, how thunderous, one can hear
the impact of every drop. But I can't lose myself in these
sensations as much as I'd like. My roof leaks, and I have
to move my bed.

The Tahitian word for woman is *vahine*, and the term
for sex is *faa hina'aro*, and, together with their French
and English equivalents, they run up a lot of mileage here.
My friend X, an anthropologist who has long pondered
the matter of love in the South Seas, made the point in
conversation yesterday that obsession with sex, which he
regards as one of the distinguishing features of Western
society, and particularly the American segment of it, does
not prevail in these regions. But after nearly two weeks in
Tahiti I have become an anthropologist of sorts myself, and
I countered by saying that, while he might be right about
the more restrained communities, it seemed reasonable to
assume, from what I had heard, that the Tahitians, male
and female alike, had hardly a thought that in some way or
other was not related to the idea of sex. Could not this be
regarded as an obsession? No, said X, and for this reason:
these people are always doing something about it, without
any feeling of guilt or shame.

I couldn't go along all the way with this, since I question that an obsession is to be defined wholly in terms of
guilt or shame, but with X's last point, that the Tahitians
are always doing something about it, one has to agree.
Little seems to have changed in this respect since the days
of the whalers and clipper ships, when the girls swam out

in their garments of tapa cloth, which soon disintegrated and fell away. I am beginning to wonder a bit, though, about the legendary beauty of Polynesian women. Perhaps I carried too many expectations in my baggage, light as I try to travel, but I find the general level of Tahitian attractiveness rather low. My first impulse was to reason that after the crews of the whalers and clipper ships had spent six or eight months at sea almost any woman would have looked pretty good, especially with the constraints of Salem and New Bedford left so far behind, but while I believe this to be more than incidental to the legend of Polynesian comeliness, I am obliged to remind myself that some things change, even in Tahiti.

By now the native stock has been thoroughly infiltrated by other strains—French and Chinese, principally, along with a few dashes of Anglo-Saxon. There is hardly a full-blooded Tahitian left on the island, and the classic Polynesian type has to be looked for elsewhere—in Samoa, for instance, where, I understand, there has been such a small amount of admixture that the island strain still predominates. One hesitates to say anything unfriendly about the Tahitians, since they are such friendly and hospitable people, but, on the whole, physically they lack distinction. Nor —and this I must admit I found surprising—do they generally live up to their reputation for gracefulness. Though they splash and frolic in the shallower waters of the lagoon, gay and full of chatter, they can't begin to touch the Hawaiians as swimmers, and, most astonishing of all, they are, in my opinion, rather poor dancers.

But if true beauty is as rare in these parts as most, I saw a girl in Papeete this afternoon who stopped me dead in my tracks. She was so beautiful, she could be appreciated as an aesthetic object, standing beyond desire. Most often, though not invariably, it seems to be the Tahitian-Chinese combination that produces the most physically becoming people on the island, and she was of this strain. She couldn't have been more than seventeen. Her skin was the color of coffee heavily laced with cream, or of one of the paler kinds of oak leaves in the fall, and a more nearly perfect set of features cannot be imagined. She was wearing a simple, badly fitting black dress, without any sleeves and cut low and square at the neck, and she had a round straw hat of local make pushed back on her head. Her brown eyes were slightly almond-shaped, her hair was glossy black, and she looked so thin and fragile that I wondered how she could possibly endure.

Nor will she long, according to a French doctor I was walking with at the time. He saw her as ravaged by tuberculosis. There is a great deal of it among the Tahitians, and, according to my informant, a fair amount of venereal disease. "But not more than in any seaport," the doctor added in a lighter tone. "Certainly not any more than in Marseille, for instance." His clinical approach reminded me of what Captain Bligh had to say on the subject in his account of the mutiny. He recorded that when the *Bounty* left Tahiti he had only two men on the venereal list and that he took this to mean that the ailment, brought to the island by the first light-skinned visitors, hadn't gained ground. Some of my acquaintances aboard the *Cloud*, however—men who spoke with what impressed me as considerable authority—had other ideas, at least as far as present-day conditions are concerned. I question whether the pleasure of their visit was in any way interfered with, but as a health resort they didn't rate Tahiti very high.

For different reasons I am coming to agree with their evaluation. I saw my first case of elephantiasis when I was out on the peninsula last week—a toothless old man with monstrously swollen limbs, lying under a mango tree—and while there are no malaria-bearing mosquitoes on the island, the ones that call Tahiti home do transmit elephantiasis, and I am beginning to wonder if perhaps I shouldn't get over some of my claustrophobic notions about sleeping under mosquito netting, an arrangement I have never been able to abide. It is reassuring to learn that there are not many cases of the disease here and that there are even fewer of leprosy, though a place is still set aside as a leper colony. On the other hand, I am told, particularly by my Western acquaintances, that everybody runs the risk of falling victim to a bad attack of boils. Worse than bad. Atrocious. One lady I know counted hers in the low forties.

My doctor friend sees the high incidence of Job's bothersome affliction as a consequence of a deficiency in diet. And it is the same lack, I imagine, that is responsible for so many Tahitians' having bad teeth. This is an affliction that appears to be more common among the women than among the men, and, without meaning to be pro-*vahine*,

I find it extremely unfair. Even with a front tooth or two missing, a man can look forward to making a reasonably long run of it, whereas the women, no matter how attractive, generally have far too short a bloom. By twenty they have begun to fade, by twenty-five they have had it, and by thirty, in most cases, hardly a sign remains of such attractiveness as they may have once possessed. The great majority start getting heavy and fat, and others, of the Tahitian-Chinese combination, begin to shrivel to sticks.

"But they take it as it comes," I was told a few afternoons ago by a French-Tahitian lady, who herself is one of the last people in the world to have any cause for that particular worry. "By then they have had children, either in or out of marriage, and, having fully enjoyed their youth, they are content to devote themselves to other things. I do not say they never wish they were young again—they are women, after all—but I know them, being in a large part of me one of them, and I do not think they grieve. They are quite realistic, even when they are young. I believe it is this, more than anything else, that will always make them something of a mystery to foreigners—North Europeans and Americans especially. It is not only that you are more complex, as some people say, but that you are so much more romantic. And this the Tahitians find hard to understand—particularly the idea of romantic love. It makes many complications."

One of the complications that this hardheaded Tahitian realism has made is evident in the pathetic misery of a young German scientist who came here about a month ago on some scientific mission or other and fell hopelessly in love with one of the prettier local girls. She was not unwilling to establish a partnership, in accordance with what is, to a greater or lesser degree, the accepted local custom, but apparently his yeasty sentimentality was more than she bargained for. Nothing is ever your own business on this island, and of late the girl's friends have chattered the affair all over Papeete, fluttering around it like a flock of sparrows. I suppose they would have to be called girls of the town, for they toil not, neither do they spin. Just before noon each day, they meet around the tables of Papeete's sidewalk café, there to drink coffee or a lemonade —rarely anything stronger—and to pick over the grains of gossip that have fallen since the day before.

What they have been saying about the young German and his girl is that he became so jealous and possessive— always asking her if she loved him and him alone, insisting on her undying devotion, falling into melancholy sulks if she so much as glanced at another man, even some old friend from the rural district where she grew up—that the girl had to simplify her life by leaving him and going to stay with an aunt in the country, again in accordance with accepted local custom. All the girls in Papeete seem to have an aunt or some other relative living in the country, and whenever anything displeases one of them too much—the source of displeasure invariably being a man—she simply ups and flounces off to this haven, knowing that she will be welcome for as long as she cares to stay, which, in most cases, is only a short time. These stormy Tahitian crises are rather like the rains.

So now, his friend having flown the coop, the young German spends the greater part of the day at a solitary table in the café, drinking beer and indulging in his own version of "The Sorrows of Werther." And though the girls at the other tables are not without sympathy and try to cheer him up, nothing can lift him out of his misery. No man could be more incomprehensible to these creatures, more utterly baffling. "But why?" I heard one of them inquire. "Are there not others? I myself would be willing to go with him. And if he does not find me to his liking, why not someone else? He is a curiosity, that man! If he wishes consolation, why will he not let himself be consoled?"

My acquaintance W, an astute Englishman who is here on a visit and who also believes the concept of romantic love to be one that these people cannot understand, interprets the girl's vexation as an indication that a strong streak of practicality runs through the Tahitian make-up, and I have since come across a case that tends to confirm his thesis. That was yesterday, while I was lunching with my anthropologist friend and his wife—an attractive young Frenchwoman who thinks of Tahiti as her spiritual home— at a Chinese restaurant midway on the road around the island. The restaurant—a large room open on all sides and covered by a corrugated-tin roof—is one of the island's popular eating places. (Its cuisine, which is more coolie than Canton, and quite unlike any Chinese food I have had elsewhere, is very good. The Chinese, by the way, are solidly established in Tahiti and have been here since well before Gauguin's time. He speaks of them in "Noa Noa." The first to arrive were brought here in 1864 to work on cotton plantations, which no longer exist, and now they have a lock on most of the retail trade in Tahiti. They own nearly all the bazaars and every last one of the little grocery stores out in the country, as well as practically all the dressmaking, shoemaking, and tailoring shops. The Papeete vegetable market is entirely in their hands, and they also control the larger part of the import business. Some of them are among Tahiti's wealthiest men.)

Yesterday was Saturday—crystal-bright after an early rain, with more flowers in bloom than ever—and the restaurant was crowded and noisy. At a table not far from us sat a good-looking, dark-haired French naval officer in uniform, certainly no older than twenty-two, and a particularly attractive girl, who wore what I have come to recognize as conventional Tahitian street attire—sandals, a flower behind one ear, a loose, full cotton skirt with a colorful floral design, and the scantiest of halters made of the same material. Aside from that fragile beauty on the streets of Papeete, whom I have been thinking of as a Tahitian Camille, the naval officer's companion was the prettiest girl I had seen on the island. I thought she looked troubled, however. She sat there quietly with downcast eyes, evidently sharing some sorrow with her young man, who was silent and seemed equally disturbed.

X and his wife knew all about them. The young officer's tour of duty on the island has come to an end, and he is

due to leave for France on the next ship. He and the girl
have been maintaining an establishment, and this is their
last week together. So along with a Tahitian Camille, I
thought, I now had a Tahitian Madame Butterfly on my
hands. But when I suggested this parallel, Mme. X shook
her head. "No, no!" she said. "You are feeling sorry for the
wrong one. He cannot marry her and take her back to
France, as he would like to—his family is very strict and
conservative, and he would be disinherited—so it is he who
will suffer from a broken heart."

"And not the girl?" I asked.

"Absolutely not!" interjected X, who sometimes gets a
bit impatient with what he calls my American prejudices.
"She will recover in two or three weeks, and in a month or
so she will have reached an agreement with another man.
These people simply do not indulge in the usual forms of
Western sentimentality. They are not like that at all."

I found this a bit emphatic, but since the Xs have lived
here for ten years and I for just over a fortnight, who was
I to argue? Yesterday evening, however, while I was visiting the Ys, I brought the matter up. Mme. Y is the cultivated half-French, half-Tahitian woman who first explained Polynesian realism to me. She and her husband,
one of the few Americans who have business interests in
Tahiti, agreed completely with the Xs about the girl in the
restaurant, except that Y was inclined to put it in stronger
terms. "Three weeks?" he said. "She will be over it in three
days. As a matter of fact, she already has a man waiting."

He smiled at his wife, and his voice took on a teasing, affectionate tone. "Good-by, hello. That's the way they are."

Mme. Y gave a little cry of protest and then frowned. But if she had wanted to put in a demurrer, she changed her mind. "And why not?" she said with just a trace of defiance, all her island loyalties coming to the fore. "That man has not been good for her. He is so jealous, she might as well have been locked up in prison. The new one will be much better for her, much better. And why should she be expected to put on mourning? She deserves her years of being young."

The girl who couldn't put up with the moody German and the girl I saw in the Chinese restaurant are only two of many who have entered into convenient arrangements with European men. In no way are they *déclassées*. They move without prejudice in the highest circles. In terms of reputation, they have something of the status of movie stars or, if we go back to the Paris of Louis Napoleon, of the great courtesans. But our Nanas and Lorettes are special cases. Papeete has its own equivalent of the Moulin Rouge and of Mabille, the Parisian dance hall where the cancan was invented, and on this level things are generally arranged on a purely commercial, pay-as-you-go basis—at least where the non-native white man is concerned.

An intelligent, well-bred Australian girl I've met, who is here for a few weeks, finds this aspect of the Parisian scene rather chilling. "You mean they do it for *money?*" she said, sounding more hurt than shocked, as if some cherished fancy had been betrayed. The temptation was to spare her, and again, not to say anything that might sound unfriendly, but though it may be argued that money is not necessarily involved—a present will suffice, such as a fan, a pair of slippers, or four yards of cloth to make into a dress —it cannot be said that material considerations do not play their part.

A Tahitian *manqué* who used to visit New York from time to time—a member of one of America's oldest families, who came here to live in 1912 and died only a few weeks ago—once grew choleric on the subject in my presence. We happened to be dining at the Yale Club, and I remember thinking it strange to be talking about the *vahines* of Tahiti in that temple of American accomplishment. "The way it is now," my companion said, "they look upon the white man as a meal ticket. Their mothers have taught them to think that way. It was different before the tourists came." The man was a scholar—an authority on Polynesian linguistics—and since he spoke from nearly fifty years of experience, I suppose there is little point in my taking exception to his remarks. It has occurred to me since, however, that he might have been putting too much blame on the tourists. I can understand how the relatively tourist-less Tahiti of 1912 must have seemed like Paradise Lost to him that night at the Yale Club, but I think he was skirting the issue. Even in the days of Captains Wallis and Cook, the girls had a practical outlook. They demanded payment in nails, of all things, and stern measures had to be taken lest the men dismantle the ships in their enthusiasm.

If I have made Papeete sound like a glittering, worldly place—the 1860 Paris of the South Seas—I had better back up a little. The town is pretty much on the grubby side, badly in need of a whitewing crew, and though it has an overlay of European civilization—automobiles and Vespas, bars and night clubs, radios and jukeboxes—it is still a trading post, and a comparatively primitive one at that. And I now realize that, beneath their thin European veneer, the Tahitians are still a rather primitive people, as my anthropologist friend X has been insisting right along. I became convinced of this over the past weekend while attending a big Saturday night at a native dance hall called the Lafayette. It stands in a grove of trees out in the country, several miles from Papeete, and, like the Chinese restaurant where I had lunch, it is no more than a large floor covered by a tin roof. It has a crude bar, serving beer and soft drinks only; long plank tables and benches arranged along three sides; and, to the right of the bar, a small platform where a four-piece Tahitian band—piano, snare drum, and two guitars—plays native music, the musicians' conception of American jazz, and a good deal of bastard calypso.

I went to the Lafayette with X, his wife, and a guest of theirs. We had purposely lingered over our coffee and brandy in the dining room of the hotel and didn't arrive until a few minutes past midnight. The place can comfortably accommodate around a hundred and fifty people, but by then more than twice that number had crowded in. Ours were the only white faces in the lot. The crowd consisted mainly, but far from entirely, of young people. The middle-aged group was well represented, and there were a few spectators long past their prime—stooped, wrinkled, practically toothless—but just as full of the spirit of the evening as anyone.

Room was made for us at one of the tables, and it took me a little while to shake loose from one environment and enter another. The place was dimly lit, the band was playing a Tahitian song called "To Reo Iti Maru" (in English this comes out approximately "Your Dear Quiet Voice"), a dozen girls had climbed up on the platform and were singing with the band, the floor was packed with dancing figures, and, without exception, all the people in the place, men and women alike, and including the musicians and the bartenders, were loaded down with flowers—leis, blossoms worn behind an ear, and wreaths of other blossoms in the hair. Even if I had been inclined to worry about being an intruder, as I wasn't, my worry wouldn't have lasted long. In my comings and goings over the past three weeks, I have become acquainted with a number of Tahitians who live in the country, and all of them were making a night of it at the Lafayette. So were many of the Xs' friends, who must make up a sizable part of the population, and long before our first round of drinks arrived we had been welcomed, bedecked, and otherwise consolidated with the others.

One thing I will always remember—those flower-laden girls, in their bright garments, singing with the band. They were completely lost in the music; nothing else existed for them. They sang and sang and sang. Jazz and calypso soon fell by the wayside, and only native tunes were played. I don't know enough about music to describe these adequately, but I do know that they were wild, savage, barbaric rhythms. And the dancing fell in line. The Tahitians have a lot to learn about Western-style dancing, but I doubt whether they are the least bit interested in it. Although they go through the motions affably enough, having a good time, it is only when they turn to their own dances that they truly come alive. All these dances fall into a single pattern, amatory and explicit—they couldn't be more explicit—though the bodies of the dancers never touch. I admit that for a few minutes I was slightly aghast. The most astonishing thing, however, is the lightheartedness of it all—a paradoxical quality of innocence. There is none of that controlled tension, so often threaded with undercurrents of brutality, that invests the gypsy flamenco; none of the sullen sexuality that characterizes the voodoo dances of such places as Haiti and Brazil; and certainly none of the predatory grimness that suffocates the dance palaces of Broadway. It took me only a short time to realize that what I was watching was a folk dance, primitive and uninhibited, but also *good-humored* and, on the whole, setting forth the proposition that sex is really not worth making too much of a fuss about.

It can get confusing, the way the past cuts across the present on this island. Take T, for example. She has gone to school, rides a motor-bike, wears a bikini when swimming, and seems in every respect a modern Tahitian girl. Yet after lunch today, when I proposed that we investigate the barrier reef in an outrigger that has been put at my disposal, she drew back and declined. Bad luck, she said. I could hardly believe my ears, since I had imagined that the taboo prohibiting a woman from getting into a canoe had died out generations ago. But T would have none of the outrigger. We settled for some sun instead.

As we talked, I tried to get T to tell me about some of the other local superstitions, but she was more interested in the gossip that has become attached, like barnacles, to some French and American motion-picture people who are making a film here. I did manage, though, to bring the conversation around to an old man who died a slow death out in one of the country districts not long ago after digging up a tiki, or stone image, in the course of planting a small banana tree. Even the intervention of a sorcerer, I had been told, couldn't save him. The sorcerer lives in a village not far from the peninsula, and T chatted about him the way a suburban housewife in the United States might talk about Dr. Spock. I said I would like to meet the sorcerer, who seems to have a wider practice than most of the local Europeans suspect, and asked T if she would introduce me. She would have none of that, either. From the look on her face, I surmised that she thought I was fooling around with dynamite.

The story of the old man and the tiki is too good to lose. His name was Tuteata Hoire, and he lived on a small plot of land that adjoins the property of the Ys. Though he was well into his seventies and remembered many of the songs and legends that most Tahitians have forgotten, he always said, whenever he was asked his age, that he was over thirty. This is the stock reply of many natives who are no longer young. According to Mme. Y, who knows them as well as anyone, thirty is the year that seems to mark their coming to maturity. Their youth is over, they know they must fall behind in the race, and after thirty, in terms of excitement and adventure, there isn't a great deal they can look forward to.

Being so old, Tuteata Hoire had outlived three wives. But still he had notions. He once proposed to the Ys' cook, who sent him packing, and he wasn't above making remarks to the young girls who walked along the beach in the evening with flowers in their hair. The old man was well liked, however, and, since he lived alone, Mme. Y tried to keep an eye on him. "He used to come to our place three or four times a week," she told me. "He liked to watch the sunset from our beach. He would always be neat and clean, wearing fresh clothes, and he was never without a flower behind an ear. He was a nice old man, really."

Tuteata Hoire was a weaver of palm thatch. He earned enough from his trade to make an occasional purchase at a neighborhood grocery store kept by a Chinaman, but for most of his food he depended on his small plot of land, less than half an acre. One afternoon Mme. Y saw him going about his work as usual, planting a small banana tree, and then five or six days passed without her seeing him again. Sensing that something was wrong, she walked over to his little two-room house, where she found him stretched out on a couch, staring at the ceiling. "I was shocked," she said. "He looked so ill that I thought he was about to die. At first he wouldn't speak to me, much less answer the questions I put to him. But after much coaxing I got him to tell me what had happened. He said he had done a bad thing, a very bad thing."

While he was planting the banana tree, Tuteata Hoire's spade happened to strike what he thought was a stone. Digging deeper, he uncovered a pinkish-red tiki, crudely carved in the shape of a woman. He knew that it was an old tiki, made long before any white men came to Tahiti, and that the name of the woman it represented was Vahina Ura. The simplest English translation is "The Red Woman," but Tuteata Hoire, in telling Mme. Y of the incident, used the phrase "The Woman of Flame." Merely to have disturbed the tiki could bring bad luck, as Tuteata Hoire knew. He hastily reburied it and planted the banana tree in a different place. "That could have been the end of it," Mme. Y said, "but unfortunately it wasn't."

Tuteata Hoire brooded upon the tiki for the rest of the day. And that night, when he fell asleep, Vahina Ura came to him in a dream. His first response was one of terror— mortal men were not permitted to gaze upon these women of the old mythology: nothing could be more taboo. However, he saw that there was a smile on her face and that her eyes were warm and kind. "She was ever so beautiful," he told Mme. Y. "Oh, but she was beautiful." Dazzled,

Tuteata Hoire neglected his work the next day and did not go down to the beach to watch the sunset. Vahina Ura again came to him in a dream that night and also the next night, and on the night following she brought a lei of *tiare Tahiti*, which she placed around his neck. She asked Tuteata Hoire to dance with her, and the years fell away. He was young once more, strong and handsome. "We danced our island dances," he told Mme. Y, "and the dances of the white man, and then——" The old man averted his eyes. "Then we did things that were bad."

During that night of dancing and taboo love, Tuteata Hoire told Vahina Ura how beautiful she was. Smiling faintly, she said that she had a daughter who was far, far more beautiful than she. And when Tuteata Hoire protested that this was impossible, her smile became sly; she promised to bring her daughter the next night, so that he could see for himself.

"What I believe," Mme. Y said, "is that, for Tuteata Hoire, the night had become more important than the day. And all this time, remember, for four days, he had not eaten. Next morning he prepared for his guests. He cleaned his little house in every corner and filled it with flowers. He put a bowl of fruit upon his table. He made two leis. After he bathed, he put on his best *pareu*, or sarong, and waited for the night to come."

As she had promised, Vahina Ura brought her daughter. The two women were accompanied by strains of music that seemed to fall from their persons. Tuteata Hoire saw immediately that Vahina Ura had spoken truthfully and that

167

the daughter was indeed more beautiful than she—a strong young girl with smooth limbs and eyes dark as the lagoon at midnight. Tuteata Hoire placed the leis around their necks, fed them fruit, and danced with them. He danced first with the daughter and then with Vahina Ura, and they all three danced together, again doing things that for a mortal man were taboo. "I shall die," Tuteata Hoire said. "I know I shall die."

Against the old man's wishes, Mme. Y sent to Papeete for one of the doctors. Tuteata Hoire said that no doctor could help him, least of all a white one, but when the physician arrived he allowed himself to be examined. Except for what could have been the beginnings of malnutrition, the doctor could find nothing wrong with the old man. Actually, everything considered, he was in extremely good condition. The doctor would have been willing to let it go at that, but Mme. Y insisted that Tuteata Hoire be taken to the hospital. After ten days there, he was sufficiently recovered to start making remarks to the nurses. Mme. Y went to Papeete and drove him home.

"The next morning it rained," Mme. Y remembers. "It wasn't a big rain, not one of our torrents, and I enjoyed listening to the sound it made on the thatch. I was arranging some flowers when Tuteata Hoire's nephew came to the door. He had taken the bus from Papeete to visit his uncle. He told me that Tuteata Hoire was very sick again and wanted to see me immediately. You cannot imagine the change. The old man seemed to have collapsed overnight. There was a dull, dead look in his eyes, and his voice had shriveled to a croak."

Tuteata Hoire was now anxious to tell what had happened—Vahina Ura and her daughter had visited him again. They were furious that he had deserted them by going to the hospital in Papeete, Vahina Ura especially, and Tuteata Hoire drew back in fear. They were so beautiful, however, and so warm and kind after their anger was spent, that he forgot his fear. So that night was like the other nights. Tuteata Hoire danced with the daughter and with Vahina Ura, and once more they did things that for a mortal were taboo. There was only one person who could help him, Tuteata Hoire told Mme. Y—Tahua, the sorcerer. He wished to visit Tahua without delay. "How could I refuse?" Mme. Y told me. "I sent word to my husband, who came around in an old station wagon we have, and we drove Tuteata Hoire to the sorcerer's village. This Tahua, the sorcerer, is a rather short, strong-looking man in his middle age. How much trade he has is hard to say. Often, however, there are rumors that someone or other has been to him. To visit Tahua, and keep it a secret, would not be easy."

Mme. Y paused for a moment, gathering her thoughts. "And now a strange thing," she said. "I believe I know the explanation, but still it was strange. Tahua the sorcerer knew all that had happened to Tuteata Hoire. Perhaps the old man told it to one of the other natives when he was in the hospital, or to a nurse, or perhaps to his nephew—one will never know."

Those who imagine a sorcerer should look like one would have been disappointed in Tahua. He wore a white shirt and dark trousers and a pair of leather sandals. "It is well you came to see me," he said to Tuteata Hoire, "for Vahina Ura and her daughter are very angry with you. You danced with them, and did other things as well, and now they feel that you want to forsake them. In the anger you have caused them, they would do you great harm." At this, a spasm of fear crossed the old man's face, and his mouth began to tremble. "But do not be afraid," said Tahua. "There are ways of taking away their mana. We must return to your house at once. I will spend the night with you, and in the morning we will do the things that have to be done."

What transpired that night between Tuteata Hoire and Tahua, no one has ever learned. When the first light of morning shone in the sky, they were seen to leave the house. Mme. Y and her husband watched from a distance, and the natives of the neighborhood, as well as many others who had come from farther away, hid in the bushes and behind the trees. Seeing Mme. Y, Tahua motioned her to join him, and explained what he proposed to do. He said first they must find the tiki of Vahina Ura, and then the tiki of the daughter—never had the one been placed into the earth without the other. And when they were found, he would take away their mana.

Tuteata Hoire led Tahua to the exact spot where he had reburied the tiki of Vahina Ura. However, search as they might, they could not find the tiki of the daughter—as the

natives said at the time, and say even today, the daughter
of Vahina Ura kept running away. Tahua spaded first in
this place and then in that, digging until the sun was high
in the sky, but always Vahina Ura's daughter kept running
away.

At noon Tahua called a halt. The daughter's tiki was
not truly important, he said, speaking to Tuteata Hoire in
Mme. Y's presence. The daughter had little power of her
own, and even this was derived from Vahina Ura: take
away the mana of Vahina Ura, and the mana of the daughter would also be dissolved. Tahua asked Tuteata Hoire if
he believed and trusted what had been said, and after the
old man replied that he did, Tahua proceeded to take away
the mana of Vahina Ura.

He bore the tiki of Vahina Ura to a nearby brook, followed by Tuteata Hoire and Mme. Y. He bathed the tiki
in the running water, speaking various incantations in the
old Tahitian tongue, and then, using a fresh white cloth,
he wiped the tiki until it was dry. "Now her power is gone,"
he said to Tuteata Hoire. "No longer can she harm you.
But you must not keep her in your house. You must give
her to someone you trust as a friend, passing her from your
hand to the hand of your friend. Do you have such a
friend, Tuteata Hoire?"

The old man looked at Mme. Y. "She is my friend. I
will give Vahina Ura to her."

He handed the tiki to Mme. Y, who thanked him for his
gift, and those who had hidden in the bushes and behind
the trees began to disperse. Tahua the sorcerer departed,

and Tuteata Hoire returned to his house, accompanied by his nephew. But the very next morning the nephew came running to Mme. Y's house and implored her to hurry to Tuteata Hoire. Mme. Y found the old man lying on his cot with a lost, despairing expression on his face. "Alas," he said, "I am going to die. I have known it ever since we could not find Vahina Ura's daughter. Tahua the sorcerer is a wise man and knows many things, but not all. The daughter came to me last night. She blames me for the loss of Vahina Ura, and there is no hope for me. I must surely die." Before Mme. Y could reply, the old man spoke again. "I wish you had come a few minutes earlier," he said. "A pair of love terns flew into the house and sat on my bed. I called my nephew's attention to them, but he could not see them. He only became frightened. And now they have flown away."

Of all the birds in the world, love terns are among the most beautiful. Not much larger than robins, they are white as snow. Because of their whiteness and the wraith-like airiness of their flight, they are sometimes called ghost terns, and fairy terns also. They fly in pairs, so close together that their wings seem to touch, and any movement of the one is matched at that same instant by a similar movement of the other.

"I wish they hadn't flown away before you came," Tuteata Hoire said to Mme. Y. "They were the whitest, most beautiful love terns I have ever seen."

In another five minutes Tuteata Hoire was dead, and now his house stands empty. The porch is crooked, the roof is falling in, and the little patch of land on which it stands is overgrown with weeds. Mme. Y still has the tiki of Vahina Ura and occasionally shows it to visitors. One of her visitors, an American, spoke rudely of it, saying that the face was evil and obscene, and for the next twenty-four hours all sorts of things went wrong for him. The rain soaked his bed, he lost some money, and he was almost carried out to sea in an outrigger. But that, of course, was pure coincidence.

Professor M is a stout, amiable man in his fifties who lives in Papeete, where he teaches Tahitian at the island's most advanced educational institution, roughly comparable to a junior college. Born in Tahiti of German parents, he is married to a Tahitian woman and has a large family —seven boys and three girls. Besides teaching classes, he gives private lessons and is compiling a Tahitian grammar. Lately I have taken to dropping by to see him, and while chatting with him this afternoon I said that I found it surprising that elementary Tahitian had to be taught in Papeete. It was as though Parisians had to be instructed in French, I observed.

The Professor shook his head soberly. "You have no idea how corrupt our language has become," he said. "In large part, the trouble is traceable to our Chinese. Just as they sometimes speak what you call pidgin English, so do they speak pidgin Tahitian. And our young people follow their lead. We actually have two languages now—one that we use with the Chinese and one that we use among ourselves.

But more and more the Chinese version is taking over—a truly lamentable decline. In my classroom, I have to start with the most rudimentary principles, as if I were teaching a foreign tongue. Sometimes I feel that Tahitian—true Tahitian—is on the way to becoming a dead language, like Latin or Greek."

As if in need of cheering up, the Professor poured us each a drink of Scotch. "Things are no longer the same in Tahiti," he said. "To a man like yourself, a visitor from the outside world, our island must seem a remote place, untouched by what is happening elsewhere. But this is not altogether true. In one way or another, we are constantly reminded that we, too, are part of the present century. In Tahiti, just as in the rest of the world, a great transformation began to occur in 1914. With us, as with Europe and, I suppose, the United States, the First World War marked the beginning of significant change. We became divided along political and class lines, and now we are always quarreling among ourselves."

Professor M paused long enough to sip from his glass. "And you take the young people," he said. "Their only interest is in having a good time, or what they call a good time—the noisy, beer-drinking life of Papeete. The girls amuse themselves with the sailors, and the young men have become indolent and soft. Life is too easy for them. The sun shines every morning, there is always something to eat, so why worry?" After draining his glass, he continued. "It is true what I said, my friend. Proper Tahitian is on its way to becoming a dead language. But lately I've read in the papers from France that they are having their troubles too—all those words being taken into the language from English and American. Well, so it goes—a world-wide decline. Here, let me freshen your glass. Whisky is becoming one of my weaknesses. It may be my own form of protest against the younger generation, but I am losing my taste for beer. Ah, if only they knew how to *speak!* I could forgive them almost anything if they did."

Today I paid another call. I believe I would have recognized my host anywhere as an American of Anglo-Saxon stock, a man of cultivation and breeding, but I was mildly surprised when he identified himself as a graduate of one of the Ivy League colleges, class of 1923. He came out to Tahiti in the autumn of that year, he said, and stayed. Married to a Tahitian woman, he lives in a spacious, pleasant house on the outskirts of Papeete, and not once in the thirty-six years that he has been here has he returned to the United States.

It amuses this man to poke fun at himself and the corrosive effects of his exile. "Who is Vice-President now?" he asked me over a cup of coffee. "No, don't tell me. It's Nixon, isn't it? He's Vice-President, and Eisenhower is President. But who in the world is somebody named Svenson, or Benson? Do you know who was in Washington in my day? Well, Harding was President, and Calvin Coolidge was Vice-President, and Will H. Hays was Postmaster General. The rest I can't remember, and why I remember Will H. Hays I'll never know. He was hardly a commanding figure. I still had a few months in the States after Coolidge became President—cutting his milk teeth, you might say; and wasn't there some joke about his having been weaned on a pickle?—but I missed Herbert Hoover and all those interminable years of Roosevelt. Did you *have* to keep him in office that long? Out here it seemed an eternity. The last book I read in the States was 'Black Oxen,' by Gertrude Atherton, and one of the last movies I saw was 'Grandma's Boy,' with Harold Lloyd. Whatever became of Norma Talmadge? I never see an American newspaper, and Tahiti doesn't publish a newspaper. I used to like Lon Chaney, Douglas Fairbanks, Buster Keaton, and Chester Conklin. Some of my friends have short-wave radios, but I haven't, and though I see an occasional copy of *Time* or *Life*, it's like reading 'Peter Rabbit.' Matter of fact, I'd *rather* read 'Peter Rabbit.' Do you remember Nita Naldi, and is it true that American men now do the dishes? Incredible!

"We have a movie theatre in Papeete, but practically all we get is Westerns—terrible Westerns. One of the best pictures I ever saw was 'The Covered Wagon.' Every two years I make a trip to New Zealand. It's the only time I ever get a chance to see any good movies. I stay for ten days, and I take in two shows a day—one in the afternoon and one at night. The pictures I enjoy I see twice. I'm leaving for New Zealand in a few days. I go there only in summer, you can bet your boots, and even then I sometimes shiver with the cold. Go back to the States? How could I? Those ghastly American winters, and men doing the dishes? It's bad enough when I go to New Zealand. Not that men do the dishes there. God forbid! Anything less than seventy-five degrees and my teeth begin to chatter. But it does give me a chance to go to the movies. Have you seen any good ones lately?"

Except for a trip to town this morning to check on my plane reservations, I've been hanging around the bungalow all day, as torpid as one of the lizards in the roof. We are having one of the hottest spells yet—ninety or more in the shade, and no sign of a breeze. Everything broils. Right now it is four o'clock in the afternoon. Looking out of my front window, I can see the surf curling over the reef, a solitary gull fishing, and a native boy in an outrigger, paddling past in slow motion. I'm too lazy even to go for a swim. I haven't shaved, and I'm back to wearing a towel. Perhaps it is just as well that I leave day after tomorrow. If I stayed here two weeks longer, I'm not sure that I'd care to pull up stakes. I've found a house farther back in the country I could move into—nothing fancy, but just the right size—and it wouldn't be hard to go native.

For those who are susceptible to Tahiti, it is like a slow, narcotic-induced illness. You can feel it getting into your bloodstream little by little, accompanied by a gradual slowing down, mental and physical, and soon you start to wonder. What difference does it make? Suppose you *do* go to pot—are there not worse disasters? What is so important about the assertive, egotistical I? Easy does it. Think of all that rush, rush, rush. Is there a more beautiful place in all the world? But these are merely the first symptoms of the illness. I have been making a study of it, drawing on such case histories as are available, and I gather that it takes about six months for the initial phase to run its course. After that a restlessness apparently sets in—a hankering to hear a concert, to see the morning paper, to go bowling, if you like bowling, or to play pinochle, if you like pinochle, to mingle with your own kind and enjoy the stimulating clash, or merely the frivolity, of matching wits.

Professor M doesn't think much of my ability to thrive on what he calls a *nourriture* of lotus. It is his idea that at the end of six months I wouldn't be able to make tracks fast enough. He cites the case of a thirty-year-old French painter of our acquaintance who is now in the median, or itchy, stage of the malaise, having come to Tahiti seven months ago. At first the young man worked hard, excited by the place and the people, and then, after the third month, he put his brushes aside. With so much beauty here to enjoy, why go through the travail of trying to create beauty? Why bother? Now, however, what originally delighted him gets on his nerves—the incessant sunshine, the sense of remoteness, the flocks of twittering girls. "These *vahines!*" he growls. "How can they be so stupid? Chatter, chatter, giggle, giggle. That's all you get. You paint a picture and they look at it, and then what? 'You have made a pink tree,' they say. Or 'Do I look like a sack of copra?' Or 'Why don't you paint something pretty?' I think of the women of Paris—so well dressed, so vivacious, so intelligent—and all I want is to smell the Seine again."

But now his money is gone, and he is tending a bar in Papeete.

According to Professor M, the young painter's whole future is likely to be decided within the next few months. "His is the crucial stage," the Professor told me. "Either he finds some way of getting back to France before his first year is out or he will never get back. That is the way it generally happens. Not always, but generally. I recall how it is with your American friend who flies all the way to New Zealand to go to the motion pictures—a delightful aberration, to my way of thinking. He may not remember how frantically restless he was after he had been here six months, but I do. And now he cannot ever live in civilization again—not even to go to the motion pictures—for more than ten days every two years."

When I arrived, I found it strange to hear people speak of "civilization" or "the outside world" in this manner, but I don't any longer. I haven't seen a newspaper since I've been here, the mail is generally a month old, and there is a constant awareness of being almost completely sealed off. I have an uneasy feeling, though, that in ten or fifteen years, if things keep going as they are, Tahiti is going to be a lost, nostalgic dream—even the far from unspoiled Tahiti of today. For what this island would like to have more than anything else is its share of the tourist dollar. American-tourist, naturally. A reputation as paradise may be fine, even if the reputation has cracks in it, but a more desirable reputation would be one like Honolulu's, with its added attraction of a Waikiki Beach. What is most hoped for is a direct plane connection with Honolulu. A new airfield, large enough for the biggest planes, is being built here, with an eye to the age of jet travel, when San Francisco and Papeete, via Honolulu, will be ten or twelve hours apart, or even less. I happened to be present at a gathering of some influential citizens at which the future of Tahiti was being discussed, and there were large, bold imaginings of a line of luxury hotels running along the shore for miles, with swimming pools, night clubs, and expensive shops—the whole tourist setup.

But not yet, anyway. The fishing gull I mentioned a while back has been joined by another, and a huge red sun is sinking into the sea. What one wants, of course, way down deep, is to be the one to take the first step onto a new, undiscovered shore. While Tahiti is a long way from that, there have been any number of times when I have been able to say, without deluding myself too much, "This is what it must be like: this is how it must feel." The evening breeze has begun to stir, somewhere a girl is singing, and a myna bird is chattering away in the hibiscus beside my porch. The scent of gardenias is everywhere.

R.L.S.

R.L.S.

NO writer could be more out of fashion than Robert Louis Stevenson is at the moment, especially in those forward echelons where he never has been much of a pet, but when I was in the South Seas and stopped off for a few hours on the island of Upolu, in Western Samoa, where Stevenson spent the last four years of his life, it interested me to find that he is still remembered affectionately by the Samoans —so much so that simply because I showed a little curiosity about him I received some of the warmest hospitality that has ever come my way.

Stevenson settled on Upolu in 1890, when he was forty years old. The bulk of his work was behind him—everything of any importance except "Weir of Hermiston," his last, unfinished, and certainly best novel—and no writer in English since Byron had become more of a legend. World-famous as an author, he had also impressed himself upon the public imagination as a flamboyant bohemian, a courageous invalid fighting a hopeless battle against tuberculosis, and a restless wanderer whose unquiet journeying had taken him from Scotland to San Francisco to southern France to Saranac Lake, New York, and finally to the South Seas.

I can't say that when I reached Samoa my mind was full of Stevenson. I had just spent a month in Tahiti, and my mind was full of Tahiti. Still, on my way from one place to the other—a trip of fifteen hundred miles, which I made by air—I entertained myself, on and off, by reading some of the letters Stevenson had written from Vailima, his estate on Upolu. The roster of his correspondents makes up a sort of court calendar of Eminent Victorians and Edwardians. Among them were William Archer, James M. Barrie, Arthur Conan Doyle, Henry James, the Countess of Jersey, Andrew Lang, Richard Le Gallienne, Sir Herbert Maxwell, George Meredith, and William Butler Yeats.

Stevenson's letters were a new experience for me. I had never looked into them before, nor had I read a full-length biography of him, and all I knew about his life in Samoa was that he went there for reasons of climate, that he persisted at his work, and that in October 1890 he sat for a pen portrait by Henry Adams.

Having only recently arrived in Samoa at the time of Adams' visit, Stevenson was living in makeshift quarters on some land he had bought a few miles outside Apia, which was then, as it is now, Upolu's largest community (its present population is fifteen thousand) and which has since become the capital of Western Samoa, currently a New Zealand trust territory. Adams was touring the South Seas with the painter John La Farge. Reaching Upolu, they called on Stevenson, and a few hours later Adams addressed himself to John Hay: "I wish you had been with us on our visit with Stevenson today. We rode about four miles up in the hills and struck a clearing covered with burned stumps with a very improvised house in the middle and a distant sea-view over the forest below. There Stevenson and his wife were perched—like queer birds—mighty queer ones too. Stevenson has cut some of his hair; if he had not, I think he would have been positively alarming. He seems never to rest, but perches like a parrot on every available projection, jumping from one to another, and talking incessantly. The parrot was very dirty and ill-clothed as we saw him, being perhaps caught unawares, and the female was in rather worse trim than the male. I was not prepared for so much eccentricity in this particular, and could see no obvious excuse for it. Stevenson has bought, I am told, four hundred acres of land at ten dollars an acre, and is about to begin building. As his land is largely mountain, and wholly impenetrable forest, I think that two hundred acres would have been enough, and the balance might have been profitably invested in soap.

"I doubt our seeing them again, but in any case we could never receive another impression so weird and grimy as this, and to add to the local color, the evening was wet and gloomy. I shall never forget the dirty cotton bag with its sense of skeleton within, and the long, hectic face with its flashing dark eyes, flying about on its high verandah, and telling us of strange men and scenes in oceans and islands where no sane traveller would consent to be dragged unless to be eaten."

Remembering this exercise in acid, I found it revealing to read, as now and then some small, forgotten island passed beneath the plane, what Stevenson had to say about Adams and La Farge. "But all our resources have not of late been Pacific," he wrote his admirer Henry James. "We have had enlightened society: La Farge the painter, and your friend Henry Adams: a great privilege—would it might endure. I would go oftener to see them, but the place is awkward to reach on horseback. I had to swim my horse the last time I went to dinner; and as I have not yet returned the clothes I had to borrow, I dare not return in the same plight: it seems inevitable—as soon as the wash comes in, I plump straight into the American consul's shirt or trousers!" (What Stevenson meant was merely that he had not yet had time to acquire a proper wardrobe, as soon he would.) Returning to the subject of Adams and La Farge, he went on, "They, I believe, would come oftener to see me but for the horrid doubt that weighs upon our commissariat department; we have *often* almost nothing to eat; a guest would simply break the bank; my wife and I have dined on one avocado pear; I have several times dined on hard bread and onions. What would you do with a guest at such narrow seasons?—eat him? or serve up a labour boy fricasseed?"

I am not trying to reconstruct Stevenson's life in Samoa, and I don't want to get drawn into side issues, but it should be noted, in relation to dining on hard bread and onions, that camping out has its disadvantages. Once his house was built and functioning, Stevenson lived, if not like a lord—which would not have displeased him—at least like the well-paid, open-handed, successful author he was.

As for Stevenson's letters in general, I doubt whether even his most devoted partisans would want to class him among the great letter writers. No more than his novels do his letters belong in the front rank. I found them wonderfully entertaining, however, and Stevenson no less appealing. It was easy to understand what his contemporaries were thinking of when they spoke of his high spirits, his generosity, his charm, and his fortitude, and why, nearly everywhere, he was regarded as the most attractive man of letters of his generation. Henry Adams, go home.

I reached Upolu on a bright, warm Sunday afternoon. During my stay in Tahiti, I had assumed that there couldn't be a more enchanting place in all the world, nor have I altogether changed my mind, but after less than fifteen minutes on Upolu I was obliged to admit, not without feelings of disloyalty, that in some respects it had an even greater appeal. Upolu is only a few square miles larger than Tahiti—four hundred and thirty to Tahiti's four hundred and two—and it is equally mountainous. But because of Upolu's considerably wider margin of coast—a good mile of it in some places, as opposed to Tahiti's practically none at all—it struck me as being much more open and spacious, even splendidly parklike, with its wide stretch of greensward where native houses clustered among palms and breadfruits and other tropical trees. Moreover, though it was summer in both places—the hot, humid time of sunshine and rain—Upolu seemed less rankly luxuriant, less breathless, less overwhelmed by the sun. But Upolu's chief appeal lay in its being so manifestly Polynesian. Stepping onto the island (my plane, a flying boat, had landed on a palm-fringed lagoon, and a launch had ferried me and my fellow passengers ashore), I waited for my luggage amid a small crowd of natives who had gathered to watch the plane come down; in Samoa, as elsewhere, it is agreeable to have something to do on a Sunday afternoon. The men wore lava-lavas—tightly belted calf-length skirts —of blue or white or, occasionally, brick-red cotton, sometimes with a shirt cut along conventional Western lines, and the women wore longer, more colorful lava-lavas, with bright cotton dresses slipped on over them. The children were garbed in the same fashion as their elders, all except one small boy, who was completely naked and was abstractedly munching on the ubiquitous chewing gum of all hot places, a sliver of sugar cane.

The official language in Western Samoa is English, but all I heard when I came ashore was the local Polynesian dialect. The men were tall and robust, standing about five feet ten, on the average, and the women, while smaller and slighter, had the same look of sturdy durability. The faces I saw were all of a light brown color and cast in the same general mold, and I could detect no trace of infiltration by any outside, non-native strain. It wasn't long before I recognized the correctness of what I had heard about the Samoans being perhaps the handsomest people in Polynesia. Tahiti began to recede in my memory as an exotic, distant corner of France where, nearly always, one is aware of the European impingement, and Upolu asserted itself as immeasurably more self-contained—*truly*, I said to myself, the South Seas.

There have been comings and goings in Tahiti ever since the middle of the eighteenth century. Samoa was practically terra incognita until around 1830. But 1830 is quite some time ago, after all, and it is the Samoans themselves who are responsible for preserving a high degree of cultural independence. Their conservatism and resistance to change are notorious. One South Seas scholar I know compares the Samoans to the less resilient of the Spaniards. He cites as an illustration the fact that whereas in Tahiti and many other places in the South Seas all the old forms of native government have vanished, in Samoa the system that prevailed long before any white people arrived—a system based on the family as the basic unit, and above that the clan—remains practically unchanged. The *matai*, the chief of a clan, is still someone to be reckoned with, and the *pelenu'u*, the village headmen, are also persons of consequence.

Having collected my luggage, I hired a car to take me the twenty miles along the coast to Apia, where I was to spend the night in a hotel. The driver of the car had a Samoan name, which I did not catch, and an English name, which was Edward. I didn't recognize the make of the automobile he drove, but there was a kind of serene stateliness about it, reminiscent of the high, roomy cabs that ply the streets of London, and over the years it had been covered with various layers of household paint—red, yellow, and blue. In any case, it ran well, and Edward was an excellent driver. He explained that he didn't own the car; it belonged to some agency or other connected with either the airline or the hotel where I was to put up. Edward and the English language were on speaking but not familiar terms. I gathered, however, that he drove the car only on plane days—an arrival and a departure every fortnight.

Edward was in his early twenties. He was tall and solid, with a heavy mop of standup hair, a blunt nose, and rather thick lips. He wore a blue lava-lava, a white shirt, and a pair of leather sandals. Since I was to be on Upolu only until nine o'clock the next morning, when my plane would fly on to Fiji, I told Edward I would like to start sightseeing as soon as I had checked in at the hotel. I said I particularly wanted to visit Stevenson's house and also the place where he was buried. It would be possible, wouldn't it?

The puzzled, groping look that crossed Edward's face made me realize he hadn't understood. "Stevenson," I said. "Robert Louis Stevenson. The one who wrote books."

Gradually Edward's expression brightened. "Ah, yes," he said. "Tusitala."

It would now have been my turn to start groping if I had not remembered that Tusitala—Teller of Tales—was the name the natives knew Stevenson by, and that in some of his letters he had used it as his signature. At first it seemed curious that he should still be known by his

Samoan name, but then it occurred to me that it would have been more curious if he hadn't been. Actually, among the Samoans, Tusitala was the only name he had.

By this time Edward and I were well on our way to Apia, riding along a paved road past one native village after the other. There are a hundred and seventy-two villages on Upolu, most of them strung along the coast, and a village may consist of as few as fifteen houses or as many as fifty. The total population of the island is approximately seventy thousand—mostly full-blooded Samoans. There are fewer than five hundred Europeans on Upolu, and not more than five thousand persons of mixed European and Samoan descent.

The villages are what make the island. Everything seems to have been done, instinctively, with an eye to the most harmonious use of space—where best to plant a palm, where best to place a house, where best to set out a clump of banana or breadfruit trees. It is as if some inspired master of landscape design had been at work. Nor have I ever seen more engaging houses. They look like old-fashioned bandstands. Each consists of a single, circular room, open on all sides, that is no more than a solid platform built of dark, volcanic stones cunningly fitted together: the platform rises five or six feet above the ground and is reached by a set of stone steps. Posts made of the trunks of palms, resting at exact intervals around the outer edge of the house, support a conical, beehive roof covered with thatch. As for size, each house could easily accommodate a band of from twenty to thirty pieces.

At my request, Edward drove at a crawl. It being Sunday afternoon, all the villagers were at home, enjoying the Sabbath after a week's not too arduous work in the fields and on the sea. Men and women were strolling about, the men clad only in their lava-lavas for the most part, the women slow and graceful in their brighter, more generous lava-lavas and knee-length dresses. Children played everywhere. As we neared one of the larger settlements, with houses on both sides of the road, Edward brought the car to a halt. "My village," he said. "Would you like to take some pictures?"

Ordinarily I leave photography to those who understand it. Even with a Brownie, I get into trouble. Now, though, I wanted to try my hand. I brought out my camera, which until then had been more or less a piece of excess luggage, and climbed out of the car after Edward. Immediately, we were surrounded by a gang of little boys. Others came running up, fleet as deer. They chattered at Edward and crowded around me. Edward, plainly displeased, admonished them in Samoan, but I was not impressed by the disciplinary effect. Some of the boys, motioning toward my camera, stood themselves in a row. A few little girls approached warily, looking shy. I took a couple of pictures of the children, and then, with Edward at my side, started to walk in the general direction of one of the houses. It stood in an open place on the side of the road nearer the sea and gave the impression of being so crowded with people that one might have supposed a family reunion to be taking place.

"Are you sure this is all right?" I asked. "Are you sure they won't mind?"

Edward nodded solemnly. "Be happy," he said. "Be very happy. My uncle's house."

Despite his encouragement, I still felt uneasy; there were too many pairs of dark, motionless eyes watching me from the house. When I reached it, I addressed myself to a short, heavy-set man who appeared, merely by the authority of his bearing, to be the head of the establishment. Barefooted, he wore a white lava-lava with a wide black leather belt and a white singlet. I asked him if I might take some pictures, and then, seeing that I was not getting through, held up my camera. He replied in Samoan and nodded agreeably. A plump woman with a pretty face, who sat on the floor beside him, and whom I took to be his wife, watched without moving a muscle. A young man came down the steps from the house and began speaking to Edward. He wore a blue lava-lava and a plaid sports shirt. Several years younger than Edward, he was very earnest and grave, carrying himself with dignity. "My cousin," Edward said, introducing us, and then, indicating the older man, added, "His father, the chief."

Not counting the chief and his wife and son, there were eight persons in the house—three men, two women, and three children. All of them but the children, who were standing around, were sitting on the floor. What had caused me to think that the house was unduly crowded was that they were all grouped near the stone steps. Largely to cover my uneasiness, I brought out a pack of cigarettes. The women declined to smoke, but each of the men accepted a cigarette readily. One of them, sitting cross-legged on a lumpy cushion, was a gaunt, wrinkled, tattooed ancient whose tattooing had been done so long ago that it had turned dark green. His lava-lava was caught up and twisted about his waist in such a way as to form a pair of tight knee-length trunks similar to those worn by pugilists of the John L. Sullivan era, and I could see that his green, complicated tattooing covered nearly the whole of his body. It gave him a slightly mythological appearance, half man and half reptile.

Lighting up, we puffed in unison. But even though the ice had been broken, I wasn't invited into the house. I stood at the foot of the steps, in the sun. A young woman came from the sea, dripping wet and extremely pregnant, wearing only a lava-lava with a floral design on a blue background. Later I learned she was the wife of the chief's son, carrying her first child. She gave me a quick, curious glance and began to dry her hair, tossing it first one way and then the other, and rubbing it with a towel. And by now all the children in the village had gathered round, boys and girls both. They stood at a little distance and stared.

Without being too obvious about it, I was able to get a good look at the interior of the house. It was immaculately clean. Two small tables, a cupboard, and a folding screen made of bamboo were all there was of furniture. A number of cushions were scattered about, and many straw mats. There was a bowl of flowers on one of the tables, and other bowls of flowers here and there on the floor. The only unmistakably non-Samoan articles I noticed were a sewing machine and a small radio. My first impression was that such a living arrangement must be singularly lacking in privacy, for there was just the one large room. But then I noticed that a section of the room was partially screened off by a piece of blue-and-white cloth draped across a length of stout twine stretching from one of the posts along the rim of the house to a single interior post, much taller, that rose from the middle of the floor to the apex of the roof. There were several such lengths of twine, all radiating from the interior post, and it was easy to see how the room could be divided into a number of units.

After taking a picture or two, I put my camera aside. It was pleasanter to visit. The chief's son acted as interpreter. I never did learn his name or that of his father, and after a few attempts he gave up trying to learn mine, but he was much more fluent in English than Edward was. It was of interest to him and the others than I was an American, Upolu being one of the places where Americans aren't often sighted, and they were also interested to hear that I had just reached their island from Tahiti. "It is far, far away," the chief's son said. "Most of our houses have electricity. Do the Tahitians'?"

I answered that the Tahitians were not far behind, except those who lived in its remoter areas, and we talked about Tahiti for a minute or two. What most quickened the household's interest, however, was my curiosity about

Robert Louis Stevenson. I mentioned to the chief's son that Edward was going to take me to Stevenson's house and burial place, and the young man's translation of what I had said touched off an animated conversation. Though I didn't understand a word, except now and then the name Tusitala, I could tell that most of the talk was being directed toward the gaunt old man with the green tattooing. I didn't find him sinister or disagreeable to look at, but I did think he was more extravagantly adorned than a boa-constrictor. He could have been anywhere from eighty to a hundred. The chief's son said to me, "My mother's grandfather. He remembers when Tusitala was alive," and a quick piece of arithmetic told me the time sequence was in order. Stevenson died in 1894, sixty-five years ago, and a man who was eighty now would have been fifteen then.

"Did he ever see Tusitala?" I asked.

"Many times. He tells tales."

"About Tusitala? What kind of tales?"

The chief's son spoke to his father, who began to smile, and then the chief's wife, turning to the old man, who had been puffing all this time on the cigarette I had given him, addressed him volubly for a half minute or so. The young woman, having interrupted the drying of her hair to step behind the hanging of blue-and-white cloth, now rejoined us. She had changed into a yellow lava-lava with a light blue dress over it and wore a red flower behind one ear. After her partial nakedness of a few minutes earlier, she seemed for an instant, before one image gave way to another, encumbered and overdressed. She said a few words to the chief's son, in what I thought was an amused tone, and then the chief, after an exchange with his wife, spoke to the old man. I felt hopelessly out of it. I might have suspected that the old man was being teased if it hadn't been for the respect with which he was treated. And after he replied to the chief, speaking in a dry, thin voice that reminded me of autumn leaves, there was a ripple of muted, affectionate laughter.

"What he likes best is to tell about Tusitala's cigars," the chief's son explained to me. "What he says is that Tusitala had the best cigars of any white man who ever came to Upolu."

This brought me up short. What, precisely, I had expected, I don't know, but I believe I was hoping for some intimate revelation, some account of an adventure Stevenson had had, some memorable remark, some new insight into his work—some scandal, even. But in a way this was better. Famous writer though Stevenson was, his Samoan friends had never thought of him as such. The name Tusitala was bestowed because of the stories he told aloud—a favorite pastime of his—and not because of the ones he wrote for publication. Indeed, as he saw it, writing for publication was a notion the natives were unable to grasp. All their own stories, their myths and legends, had some assumed relation to fact—these were the old times, and these were the old gods, and this was what happened. But as for literary creation, "they do not know what it is to make up a story," Stevenson wrote in a letter to Conan Doyle.

Eventually, as Stevenson's lavish expenditures continued—a house built and furnished, presents given, feasts spread, visitors entertained—the natives began to think of him as a sorcerer. How else could he have acquired the large sums of money he spent? It came to be believed that he possessed a powerful talisman, perhaps even the magic bottle—a source of inexhaustible wealth—that he wrote about in "The Bottle Imp," his first Polynesian story. In some way or other the story passed into common currency; the chances are that Stevenson himself started it on its rounds. Not knowing what it was to make up a story, the natives took this one literally. "Parties who come up to visit my unpretentious mansion," Stevenson continued in his letter to Conan Doyle, "after having admired the ceilings by Vanderputty and the tapestry by Gobbling, manifest toward the end a certain uneasiness which proves them to be fellows of an infinite delicacy. They may be seen to shrug a brown shoulder, to roll up a speaking eye, and at last the secret bursts from them: 'Where is the bottle?'"

After the first jolt of hearing it said that Stevenson had the best cigars of any white man who had ever come to Upolu, I began to feel unaccountably pleased. From my session with his letters, I knew that Stevenson had plunged into Samoan politics, taking sides in a feud between two chiefs, which developed into open warfare for the control of what was then still a native kingdom. A certain Malietoa

Laupepa, backed by the Germans, who were the actual masters of Samoa at the time, was opposed by the more popular Mataafa, and Stevenson supported Mataafa. He even wrote a pamphlet, "A Footnote to History: Eight Years of Trouble in Samoa," to gain backing in the capitals of Europe for his man's cause. In a sense, it was a quixotic effort on Stevenson's part, since, for reasons too complicated to go into, both England and Germany sent warships to put Mataafa down, but I, as a Johnny-come-lately partisan of Mataafa's, considered it, quixotic or not, a splendid one. So did many Samoans, and to show their appreciation they hacked out a road through the jungle from Apia to Stevenson's house; Ala Loto Alofa, they called it—the Road of the Loving Heart.

With this in mind, I had thought that it might be as a champion of Samoan liberty that Stevenson was remembered by the natives—a Pulaski, a Lafayette, a von Steuben. But plainly, as far as my new friends were concerned, I had been wrong; champion of Samoan liberty Stevenson may have been, but here, in this house, it was the fragrance of his cigars that had kept his memory alive. I looked at the old man, as green as a boa-constrictor and, for the moment, just as still, and all of a sudden I felt that somewhere in his memory, tucked away with Stevenson's cigars, there must be a recollection, quite vivid, of his magic bottle. How, though, could I be certain? Wasn't there some way to nail it down? As I was wondering, I lost my chance. The chief spoke to his son, glancing once or twice in my direction, and the young man turned to me. "My father would like you to stay to dinner," he said. "We would be pleased to have you."

Again I was brought up short. I couldn't have been more surprised. And I wanted to stay. What I would get to eat I had no idea, and in matters of gastronomy I am not always as adventurous as I might be, but still I wanted to stay. It was ignorance that deterred me. I was afraid I wouldn't know how to behave. "I'd like to, but I can't," I said. "The afternoon is getting on, and I don't have much time. Will you thank your father for me and say how grateful I am? And one other thing. Will you tell your mother's grandfather I liked hearing about Tusitala's cigars? Say I wish I had as good a cigar to give to him."

The chief nodded understandingly as his son translated what I had said, and then the young man addressed his great-grandfather. The old man listened quietly, sitting cross-legged on his lumpy cushion, and though I knew it was only my imagination, even his eyes looked green. A few minutes elapsed before he spoke. When he finished, there was another ripple of laughter, louder and gayer. The young woman in the yellow lava-lava and light blue dress, looking at me, giggled into her hands.

"What does he say?" I asked.

The chief's son appeared half embarrassed, reluctant to answer. "What he says," he told me, "is that he likes your American cigarettes almost as well as Tusitala's cigars."

I found it so sly and sophisticated that I had to laugh. Following my example, the chief laughed also. After a moment, so did his son. Not for an instant did I know exactly what was happening, and I couldn't have felt more isolated, yet I had the impression that some moment of uneasiness had passed. The big round room was full of smiles.

"Do you think I might give him a pack?" I asked the chief's son.

"If you wish."

By the time it was over I had handed out six packs of cigarettes—my whole supply. Soon thereafter I took my leave, and Edward drove me on to Apia.

I signed in at the hotel, a raised wooden cottage facing the harbor, and started out with Edward on my Stevenson pilgrimage. It was then close to three o'clock. Our first stop was to be Stevenson's house. Edward drove down Apia's main street, which is no more than a short extension of the paved road we had taken from the seadrome, with a line of shops on one side and the beach on the other, and once again it was clearly Sunday afternoon—the shops shuttered, the street deserted, the long, slow roll of the surf breaking on the beach, and the drift of an English hymn mingling with the thick, unpleasant smell of copra. Farther along we passed several churches—I'm sure I counted five —and I remarked to Edward how numerous the places of worship seemed to be. "Many, many churches in Apia," he said. "*Too* many."

In April 1891, six months after Adams and La Farge paid their call on Stevenson, he vacated the temporary quarters his American visitors had found him in and moved into the house that, with the later addition of another wing, was to be his home for the rest of his life. "We are in our house after a fashion; without furniture, 'tis true, like the family after a sale," he wrote Edmund Gosse. "But the bailiff has not yet appeared; he will probably come later. The place is beautiful beyond dreams; some fifty miles of the Pacific spread in front; deep woods all round; a mountain making in the sky a profile of huge trees upon our left."

As Stevenson became increasingly a legendary figure back home—even today the island of Upolu is no easy place to get to, and in 1891 it was truly off at the end of the world—his house took on a legendary quality of its own. Contradictions abounded. A hovel to some, it was a mansion to others. "Neither was true," Stevenson's wife, Fanny, wrote in a preface to a new edition of "St. Ives," published ten years after her husband's death. "The house at Vailima was a plain, large wooden building, with wide verandahs and many doors and windows. We had our own furniture, linen, plate, and china brought from home, and lived very much as we would in England, with a few American innovations. To a man just off a cruise among the islands, no doubt an evening spent at the house in Vailima, with its waxed floors and antique rugs, its rooms blazing with lamps, the glitter of glass and silver, and the flower-bedecked, noiseless houseboys, would seem like a glimpse into paradise. On the other hand, a tourist fresh from the colonies or San Francisco would accept all this as a matter of course, but would note with disapproval the bare feet of our butler, and be much annoyed when the shoes, put out over night to be blacked, showed by their sodden condition in the morning that they had been washed, inside as well as out, under the garden hose."

Edward and I drove to Vailima over Ala Loto Alofa. "Much work on this road," he told me in his earnest, solemn fashion. "All by ax. No machinery in those days." The road now has a hard surface part of the way, but otherwise it can't have changed much in the past sixty-odd years. Vailima is a little over four miles from Apia, in the foothills of a range of mountains that runs like a backbone from one end of Upolu to the other. As soon as you leave Apia, the woods close in on both sides, and within minutes the silence becomes the heavy silence of the bush. At one place a bird darted across the road, flying erratically, like a dove. It veered off into the woods, and I asked Edward what kind of bird it was. "Bird," he replied. "Just bird." One thing about Edward, you could generally count on what he said.

Soon we came to a long, gently curving avenue of splendid trees leading off from the road at an obtuse angle. Edward stopped the car, and I knew where we were. Stevenson's description of his property to Edmund Gosse— "some fifty miles of the Pacific spread in front; deep woods all round; a mountain making in the sky a profile of huge trees upon our left"—needn't be changed to fit it today. Since Stevenson's time, however, the grounds have been extensively landscaped, and the house is no longer the "plain, large wooden building" that Fanny Stevenson remembered. Considerably altered, it now forms one wing of a much larger, handsomer structure called Government

House, which serves as the official residence of the High Commissioner for Western Samoa.

I didn't tarry long. Walking down the avenue of trees toward the residence, which is set in a vast expanse of that impeccably groomed lawn that seems to have followed the flag out of England to all corners of the globe, I tried to imagine the house as it had been when Stevenson lived there. I didn't do very well. I knew that Stevenson had suffered his last collapse on the front porch after a morning's work on "Weir of Hermiston," and there the porch was, but whatever investment of love and trouble he had put into his house, and even his final agony, was too far away. Vailima was merely another Government House.

It was in this slightly depressed mood that I began the climb to Stevenson's grave. He is buried on top of the mountain he wrote Gosse about, which appears on the map of Upolu as Mount Vaea. It rises sharply and steeply, achieving precisely the profile of trees that Stevenson described, but it can be called a mountain by courtesy only. A plumb line dropped from its summit to its base would measure no more than five hundred feet.

Edward declined to make the climb with me. It was just past four o'clock, cloudless, with the sun blazing down, and I believe he thought I was overdoing it a bit. Soon I was of a similar mind. The path to Stevenson's grave toils straight up. Jungle lines the path on both sides, and in some places the branches of the trees, tangled with vines and creepers, meet solidly overhead. Once, blundering about clumsily, I lost the path, and it began to seem like a totally foolish performance. I wasn't that much interested in Robert Louis Stevenson in the first place; I had been taken by his letters, and it had been entertaining to hear that sly old tattooed man tell about his cigars, but why *this?* Had I ever so much as ventured near Stratford on Avon?

The summit of Mount Vaea flattens out into a level place just large enough to accommodate Stevenson's tomb. Gaining my objective, I felt a still heavier sag of depression. Such a forlorn, forgotten, ill-kept tomb! What it looks like is an ungainly concrete coffin resting on a base of concrete blocks. The concrete is cracked and discolored, and bits have fallen away. On the tomb are three bronze tablets, one in front and one on either side. Not until I read the lettering on the front tablet did I remember that Fanny Stevenson shared the tomb; her ashes were interred there in 1915. The two remaining tablets pertain to Stevenson. One bears an inscription in Samoan, which reads, as I have since learned: "The resting place of Tusitala. Thy country shall be my country and thy God my God." The other tablet is in English. Beneath Stevenson's name and the dates of his birth and death are the lines:

Under the wide and starry sky,
Dig the grave and let me lie.
Glad did I live and gladly die,
And I laid me down with a will.

This be the verse you grave for me:
Here he lies where he longed to be;
Home is the sailor, home from sea,
And the hunter home from the hill.

I read the verses and turned away, thinking of all the things that the outriders of modernism might find wrong with them. No sprung rhythms, no footnotes, no obscure literary allusions, no foreign words or phrases. Halfway between Tennyson and Edgar Guest. Sugary as cotton candy. More of a pome than a poem. And yet . . .

Home is the sailor, home from sea,
And the hunter home from the hill.

Edward must have thought me in a bad humor when I reached the car. We drove back to the hotel without any conversation, and there I paid him off and arranged for him to call for me in the morning and drive me to the plane. I had a shower and changed into some fresh clothes, ate supper, went for a walk, and then turned in. That was that, I thought; Robert Louis Stevenson and I could now part company.

After breakfast, however, as I stood waiting for Edward in front of the hotel, the son of the chief who had invited me to dinner came pedaling down the road on a bicycle. He dismounted and we shook hands. "My father asked me to come see you," he said. "He wants me to say that we hope you will visit here again, and that when you do you will stay in our village. We would like to have you as our guest."

It could have been an empty gesture. It could have been a strict observance of formal Samoan politeness. It could even have been those six packs of cigarettes I had handed out. But I don't think so. I think it was Robert Louis Stevenson. I expressed my thanks. I said I couldn't think of anything I would like more than to stay in his village. And then, recalling that tattooed old man, and thinking of the frustration I had met with the day before, when I lost my chance to learn whether one of his recollections was the recollection of a magic bottle, I boldly spoke what was in my mind.

"Tell me something," I said. "I have read that in the old days, when Tusitala was alive, he was thought to have a magic bottle. It was supposed to give him all the money he wanted—money enough to do anything, to buy anything. Have you ever heard of this bottle? Has your mother's grandfather ever told of it?"

The chief's son looked at me in his grave, sober way and seemed to draw himself up straighter. For a moment I was worried that I had offended him, for who was I to imply that his mother's grandfather was an ignorant, superstitious savage, and this on the heels of such a generous invitation? But then, slowly and secretively, he halfway smiled. "My mother's grandfather is a very old man," he said, speaking as one emancipated villager might speak to another. "On his next feast day he will be eighty-five. All the old people are full of tales."

There Is Indeed but One Ronda

THERE IS INDEED BUT ONE RONDA

A FEW springs ago, when my wife and I were getting ready for an extended motor trip through Spain, one of the places we decided we wanted to see was the small city of Ronda. We were put on to it by Richard Ford's "Handbook for Travellers in Spain." There isn't much to say about Richard Ford except that he was one of those eighteenth- and early-nineteenth-century Englishmen who seem to have had it pretty much their own way. A barrister who never practiced, he collected majolica, built up a fine gallery of pictures, contributed at his leisure to the *Quarterly Review*, and did a lot of getting around. From 1830 through 1833 he was in Spain, traveling the country on horseback, and in 1840, at the invitation of the London publisher John Murray, who was bringing out a series of guidebooks to the various European countries, he began compiling his "Handbook." Published in 1845, it ran through six editions but now has long been out of print. I was lucky to come across a copy, however, and no sooner had I looked into it than I knew I was in the company of a man as informed and entertaining as his better-known fellow Englishman and contemporary, George Borrow. Along with being a guidebook, Ford's work is a collection of essays on various aspects of Spain, the Spanish, and their way of life—cigars, bullfights, robbers, smugglers, inns, cookery, St. Theresa of Ávila, Don Quixote, and so on. Page after page struck me as being as good as anything in Borrow's "The Bible in Spain," and some pages as even better, so when Ford gave it as his opinion that Ronda was undoubtedly one of the most picturesque places in Europe, adding, "There is indeed but one Ronda in the world," I needed no further urging.

Neither did my wife. We found Ronda on our road map and circled it in red. The circle fell across some of the highest mountains in southern Spain. Ronda, which lies southeast of Seville and almost due west of Málaga, began to look like a rather difficult place to get to. We had been given all kinds of warnings about the sorry shape of some Spanish roads, and our map tended to confirm them. As far as we could make out from its legend, all the roads that went to Ronda were either poor or bad or very bad, with the bad and the very bad predominating. Nevertheless, since we had intended to drive from Seville to Málaga anyhow, we decided to take our chances and make a detour by way of Ronda. The fact that it appeared to be more accessible by burro than by car made it seem all the more interesting as a port of call.

Our automobile was a small French one. We picked it up in Paris and drove south from there. Crossing the Spanish border at Irún, we proceeded to Bilbao, then to Burgos, Segovia, and Madrid, and from Madrid to Seville by way of Oropesa, Mérida, and a number of other small towns and villages. Though by the standards of most American drivers it isn't a particularly long journey from Irún to Seville—just over five hundred miles by the most direct route—it took us nearly a month to make the trip, but then we didn't go by anything like the most direct route, and we didn't hurry. Neither of us had ever been in Spain before, and there was so much to do and see, so much wonder and excitement, that some days on the road we didn't make fifty miles.

Three things, by the time we reached Seville, I had made up my mind about: that Spain, scenically, is the most astonishing country in Europe; that the Spaniards are among the kindliest of all the world's peoples; and that after some of the roads we had traveled, carrying us up, down, and across mountains, and around hairpin curves in dizzying descents (one day we took a wrong turning and rode for miles and miles across a high, bare, desolate moor with the snow-capped peaks of a sierra rising alongside us less than a mile away)—after such an apprenticeship we had no reason to be intimidated by what any map said about the roads to Ronda. Not much larger than a burro, our French car had proved itself just as dependable. I felt that it and we made a good team.

There was hardly a place in Spain that I didn't hate to leave, and I especially hated to leave Seville. It is the one city I know of that lives up absolutely to the advance billing of its most enthusiastic admirers. The orange trees were in bloom when we arrived, and many other flowers as well

—carnations and oleanders and geraniums and a greater profusion of roses than I had ever seen anywhere. Mornings when I'd wake to the sound of horses and hoofs and creaking wheels, for Seville is still in large part a horse-drawn city, and perhaps of a boy singing a flamenco song on his way to work (he passed our corner just after eight o'clock and almost invariably he was singing)—on such mornings I wanted to stay forever. Ronda didn't interest me nearly as much as it had back in the United States. While Ford might be right in saying that there is but one Ronda, so is there but one Seville. Why should I want to go anywhere else?

When we started driving again, however, things immediately began to brighten. What happens when you take to the road in Spain—especially when you leave the highways—is that you travel a trick of time, one that curves back several hundred years. These shepherds and goatherds, this goosegirl, this boy driving a herd of swine, this other boy tending a flock of turkeys, this green gypsy cart with the women sitting relaxed in their beads and colored garments while the men keep pace with the horse, these mountain children who pour out of their huts to see if they can run as fast as your slow-moving car, so strange is the sight of an automobile to them—where are we, and in what age, and what has happened to the centuries in between?

And then, along with the ever-changing Spanish landscape—the green valleys, the aching desolation of high fastnesses where nothing grows, the ruined castles, the forgotten villages that look like heaped-up chunks of adobe-colored earth, the chasms and gorges, the cork forests, the olive groves, the wild flowers, the shock of surprise on surprise—along with this face of Spain, there are the faces of the people you stop to talk with. These would be the men, mostly—farmers and shepherds and wagoners and laborers on the roads—and there is always time enough to take time out. "Command me," they say. "What is it that I can do?" Then, when you inquire about a distance or a direction or a place to stay, there is a sudden collapse of the severe presence with which the Spaniard confronts the world, and you notice the quick, warm desire to establish the kind of truly human communication that is based on unfailing courtesy and pride. The raggedest vagrant or poorest countryman knows that he is your equal and the equal of any man, and, in his own secret heart, that he is perhaps a little better than most— a Christian gentleman, an old and wellborn one (*cristiano viejo y rancio*)—and he conducts himself accordingly. Whatever the offenses or iniquities of its economic and political structure—and they are many—Spain is in this respect a completely classless country.

To offer such a man anything in the way of money would be as unthinkable as it would be for him to accept it. A cigarette, however, is a different matter. It performs the same service as the breaking of bread. In the country regions, the cigarette will generally be once refused before it is accepted, in keeping with the ancient canons of Spanish correctness, and when it is accepted, you smoke and chat together, and even your atrocious Spanish is for-given.

"These are fine goats you have."

"They will do."

"How many are there?"

"A hundred."

"They are fine animals. But tell me—are we far from the road that leads to Segovia?"

"No, not far. Continue straight ahead until you come to a bridge. At the bridge, you will find two roads. One goes to the right, the other to the left. Take the one to the right. It leads to Segovia. So the sign says, anyway. I have never been to Segovia myself."

"Many thanks."

"It is nothing. Are you French, may I ask?"

"No, I am not."

"English?"

"No, American. A North American."

"Ah, a North American. I have never spoken to a North American before. It is an honor."

And so, friends now, you part, and you are sent on your way with the old benedictory farewell, *"Quédese con Dios"*—"May you remain with God." You look back once, but already the goatherd has moved on. He and his kind are making their annual trek to the summer pastures, in some cases as much as two hundred miles distant.

It did not take me long, then, once we were on the road to Ronda, to get over having had to leave Seville. Since this was to be another fairly short hop—the distance from Seville to Ronda is something less than a hundred miles—we made a leisurely departure at ten o'clock in the morning. We started along the highway leading to Jerez de la Frontera, the sherry capital, but after following it for about twenty miles we abandoned it for a secondary road—in poor shape but rank and glorious with wild flowers and passing between fields of flax so blue that at first we mistook them for little lakes—which veers off in a southeasterly direction to the town of Villamartín. From there it swings first northeast and then southeast to form a wide forty-mile semicircle, which is anchored at the far end by Ronda.

This part of Spain—Andalusia, deep south—is the Tarshish of the Bible and the Tartessos of the Greeks. It could hardly be more of a slag pile of history—Phoenician, Greek, Carthaginian, Roman, Visigoth, Moorish, Christian. The Moors invaded Spain in 711 and stayed until 1492, and Andalusia was their last stronghold. From 1492 till now is practically no time at all—in Spain it isn't—and there are traces of the Moorish occupation everywhere in Andalusia. The Moors' noblest monuments, of course, are the mosque in Cordova and the Alhambra in Granada. That we knew. What we were not prepared for was the Moorish character of so many of the farmhouses—square, flat-roofed, dazzlingly whitewashed, each with an outdoor beehive oven—and the frequency of women (some walking, some riding on burros) who went completely wrapped in shawls, like veils, with only a narrow opening for the eyes. Villamartín, which is about thirty-five miles from the Seville–Jerez highway, has the appearance of an almost wholly Moorish town. The main street, leading to the town square, is flanked by solid lines of low, whitewashed houses, built one onto another, with long, narrow windows protected by heavy iron bars. There were a few children playing about, dark and Arab-looking, and when we got out of the car to walk around a bit, they followed us, just to stare. We didn't see much begging in Spain, except among the gypsies, who have made a profession of it and brought it to a pitch of refinement unmatched anywhere in the world.

I had run out of cigarettes, and we went into a wineshop to inquire the way to a tobacconist's. A radio was blaring out a flamenco song, and there were a few flyspecked posters on the wall advertising some last year's bullfights in Seville. Outside again, following directions, we passed a knot of men loafing in the square. You see them everywhere in Spain, these groups of unemployed. One of the bitter facts of Spanish life is that there simply is not enough work to go around. And what there is, is most often very poorly paid. In order to support himself and his family, a man in one of the cities may work at two or three different jobs—if, that is, he is talented enough to manage some such combination as being a schoolteacher in the morning, a guide in the afternoon, and a bookkeeper at night. The agricultural laborer is less lucky. One job is all he can hope for, and he is entirely at the mercy of the weather and the absentee landlords.

The last thing Villamartín seemed to me to need was a traffic policeman, but it had one, nonetheless. He had

taken up his station at the point on one side of the town
square where the main street is crossed at right angles by
another. He was dressed in a blue coat with tarnished
brass buttons, a pair of patched trousers, rope-soled sandals, and a cap, made of dark blue cloth, that looked something like the headgear favored by engineers and firemen
on American railroads. He appeared to be in his sixties,
and though until we showed up he had only a few burros
and bicycles to deal with, he obviously believed in his job
as much as if he had been in charge of the busiest intersection in Barcelona or Madrid. We had to drive by him
to get out of town, and when he saw us coming he gave
us the works. He seemed glad of the chance to keep his
hand in.

Past Villamartín, the road to Ronda began to climb
rapidly, and soon we were in the mountains. The road
steadily deteriorated, and we hadn't gone ten miles when
we came to realize that the makers of our map had been
guilty of the most repressed kind of understatement. In
some stretches, this was the worst road yet. Even so, it had
its compensations. The country took on a wild, majestic
grandeur that made it easy to understand why smuggling
and banditry have long been among the chief occupations
of the Rondeños. This part of Spain isn't far from Gibraltar,
and Ford, whose book is almost as pertinent today as it
was when it was written, speaks of Gibraltar as "that
hot-bed of contraband, that nursery of the smuggler." The
contrabandista isn't as much in evidence in the mountains

around Ronda as he is in Andorra, on the northern border
of Spain, where he goes about his trade more or less in
broad daylight, but I gathered that he still survives in the
south. Banditry, naturally, makes a louder noise. I didn't
hear of any recent incidents, but not more than ten years
ago the bandit business was so brisk in these mountains
that the whole region had to be policed off. It is said that
the bandits ruled over a substantial area, including several
villages. They picked up a Málaga businessman and got
a ransom of half a million pesetas, or about fifteen thousand dollars, for him. We found ourselves looking twice
at every man we passed, but, one and all, they couldn't
have been more cordial.

During most of our trip through Spain, we picnicked
along the road at lunch time. It was easier and pleasanter
than having to search out a town with a restaurant for
our midday meal. Besides, there was often no such place.
It was past noon when we left Villamartín, and on toward
one o'clock we began to look for a likely spot to spread our
lunch. We eventually found one on a grassy hillside just
beneath the high, isolated village of Zahara. I have been
unable to learn how Zahara came by its name, but offhand
it would seem that whoever christened it must have had
the Sahara in mind. Zahara is a Moorish town, one of the
oldest in southern Spain. The way it sits, perched on the
very summit of a lofty, jagged outcropping of rock—a conical peak, actually—and the way it is further protected by
a small, rushing river made it practically impregnable
prior to the invention of artillery. It rates a footnote in

history because its capture by the cannon-equipped forces of Ferdinand and Isabella in 1483 was the first major blow struck in the war against the Moors that ended nine years later with the fall of Granada and their final expulsion from Spain.

Lunch that day was bread, cheese, sardines, two oranges, wine, and bottled water. From where we sat, we could look down at the river and up at Zahara. There was a great red splash of poppies on the near shoulder of the road, with white, white daisies mixed in, and the clear mountain stream made a cool, rushing sound. Zahara might as well have been deserted. It was the interlude of the siesta, and we could see no sign of life anywhere on the peak. There comes a moment in every long sojourn in a foreign country when you seem to cross an invisible line. The accustomed and the familiar drop so completely away, and there is such a sense of release and renewal, that you are taken by the purest kind of joy. I was opening a can of sardines, trying not to cut my fingers, and my wife was slicing a loaf of bread and saying how bright the poppies were, when, suddenly, the line was crossed. I knew that I would remember this place and this moment for a very long time.

Ronda, when finally we drove into it around four o'clock in the afternoon, ran the risk of being an anticlimax. Ford, however, was right. A more picturesque place could hardly be imagined, and it is most improbable that there is anything like it in the world. To be sure, the town itself, while interesting enough, is no more so than any number of other places in Spain. What gives Ronda its uniqueness is its location. Surrounded by a magnificent distant amphitheatre of mountains, some peaks of which rise to over six thousand feet, and looking down on a wide, fertile plain that stretches for miles along their base, Ronda is built at the top of both sides of a gorge ("a stupendous rent in the mountains," Ford calls it) that is some three hundred feet wide and five hundred feet deep. Formed in ages past by the Guadalevín River, which bisects the rocky ridge where Ronda is situated, the gorge is spanned at its narrowest point by an incredible four-arched stone bridge. Resting on a basic arch that extends all the way across the gorge, a central arch rises to a height of more than a hundred feet, and at either end of this are two smaller arches, which complete the span. The general effect, when you look up at it from the bottom of the gorge, is not so much that of a bridge as of some massive yet graceful fortification. Built in 1761 from plans drawn up by an architect named José Martín Aldeguela, this structure is known as "the new bridge," because there are two other bridges farther down the river, one credited to the Romans, the other to the Moors. So splendid an achievement as the new bridge would have been enough to cause Aldeguela to be remembered in Ronda, but he further impressed his memory upon the place when he tumbled from his handiwork, shortly after its completion, and was dashed to pieces on the rocks below. The spot from which he fell is still pointed out to visitors. It is just to one side of a rather unusual feature that Aldeguela introduced into his bridge—a one-room jail, barred like a cage, that pierces the masonry directly above the keystone of the central arch. Used for the incarceration of short-term offenders, it apparently served the same purpose as the New England stocks—punishment and warning by public display. In Ford's time, and for some years thereafter, one of the Rondeños' favorite forms of entertainment was strolling to the bridge for a look at the prisoners. This diversion is no longer available.

Here, though, I am anticipating a bit. I am telling of things that I did not learn until later. Before we left Seville, I had made a reservation at the hotel in Ronda, which turned out to be needless forethought. The hotel, when we checked in, had an empty, deserted appearance—that and a kind of faded, spacious gentility, what with its parlor, lounge, library, cardroom, and bar, and several lesser public rooms tucked away here and there. Two stories high and of wood construction, with a wide piazza looking down on a garden arranged in the English fashion—borders of calendulas, daisies, larkspur, and roses: beyond doubt a truly lovely garden at one time but now hard pressed and discouraged by the weeds—the hotel, in its ambition, seemed to have considerably overreached itself. I wondered when it was built, and by whom, and why it had been planned on such an enthusiastic scale.

A pair of extremely agreeable boys, a tall one and a short one, showed us to our room. They wore what once had been uniforms—once, I say, because it was only by their highly polished brass buttons that we could recognize them as such; made of some blue material that was

faded, patched, and worn almost through, they had the
indifferent fit of hand-me-downs. Our room had also seen
better days. It was spotlessly clean, but there was the
same forlorn look about it (flowered wallpaper yellow with
age, a bedside lamp with a frazzled cord and torn shade,
carefully darned rips in the lace curtains) that I had by
now come to associate with every aspect of the hotel.

A small wooden balcony opened off our room, and when
we stepped out onto it, there was the Ronda view—the
stern sierras in the distance, with nearer foothills terraced
to their very tops, the green plain, and the foaming river
in the stupendous chasm of the gorge. We asked the boys
to bring us some coffee, and sat on the balcony, looking.
It was an hour before we decided to take a walk around
the town.

In a sense, Ronda's history goes back to Roman times.
About eight miles to the northeast is a hamlet called
Ronda la Vieja, which contains the ruins of a Roman theatre. (Spain is littered with more Roman antiquities than
any other country except Italy. A number of them are almost as good as new, like the ramparts in Tarragona and
the third-century aqueduct, ten miles long, that is still
used to provide Segovia's water supply. The ruins in Ronda
la Vieja are more on the ruined-ruin side.) In Ford's day,
some authorities believed that Ronda la Vieja stood on the
site of the Roman town of Arunda, which some other authorities believed took the place of an even earlier Roman
settlement, called Acinipo. Though there seems to be a

good deal of confusion about the whole matter, since both Pliny and Ptolemy made Arunda and Acinipo two different places and since the current informed consensus is that, whether one place or two, they were in any event farther north, it appears almost certain that when the Moors took over Spain they used Ronda la Vieja as a source of building material for Ronda. Various inscriptions discovered on bits of old stone in Ronda pretty well clinch the matter.

As it stands today, Ronda is actually two towns—a Moorish one, dating back to the eighth century, on one side of the gorge, and, on the other, a Spanish one, which was built up during the fifteenth and sixteenth centuries, after the Moors, reduced by a siege that lasted twenty days, surrendered the city to the armies of Ferdinand and Isabella in 1485. (It was during this siege that iron cannon balls were used for the first time in Spain; the ones that did for Zahara were made of stone.) The hotel where we put up is in the Spanish town.

When we started on our walk, it was past five o'clock and we didn't feel up to any real sightseeing. All we wanted was to get a general idea of the place. Before leaving the United States, I had been surprised to learn that Ronda's population was put at more than eighteen thousand in Ford's time and at thirty thousand by the most recent census. My inclination, as we made our way toward the center of town, would have been to put the figure at eight thousand at the outside, but in this, as subsequent exploration disclosed, I would have been wrong. Ronda stretches along its ridge for nearly a mile. The ridge knifes up sharply on the Moorish side of town, where in some places its builders had hardly room enough to squeeze in a couple of narrow parallel streets, but on the Christian side of the bridge things aren't so crowded; at its widest point, this section of Ronda is seven blocks across. A population of thirty thousand still seems generous to me, but, considering that the place is jam-packed and that the people who live in the surrounding countryside are also included in the figure, I am willing to admit that the census takers know more about their business than I do.

Spoiled by some of the other places we had seen in Spain, we were not at first much taken with Ronda itself. While it is true that there are few Spanish towns where one is not reminded of the poverty of the nation, the streets of Ronda, especially in the shopping district, seemed not only poor but mean. Again needing cigarettes, I steered my wife into a tobacco shop, and we fell into conversation with the proprietor. The only generalization that can be made about the physical appearance of the Spaniards is that they are more often short than tall, more often swarthy than fair-complexioned, and more often brunette than blond. The tobacconist was part of the minority. He was also thin and blue-eyed and had a long, narrow, bony face. It turned out that he could speak English. He told me that he had picked it up as a young man while working in a draper's shop in Algeciras. "It is near to Gibraltar, and many of the English go there frequently," he explained. "An English lady took an interest in me and helped me to learn her language. She gave me a book to learn from. It was John Bunyan's 'Pilgrim's Progress.' I did not find it sympathetic, but this, of course, I never said to her."

My wife left to do an errand, and I remained to talk with the tobacconist. I asked him what the people of Ronda did to make a living. After shrugging his shoulders as if to say that making a living in Ronda was not the easiest of propositions, he told me that farming was the main standby. The larger landowners contracted for labor on a day-to-day basis. There were a number of orchards and vineyards and a considerable amount of animal husbandry—cattle, mules, horses, burros, goats, and pigs—but even so there was never enough employment to go around. Then, too, some of the jobs that used to be available had lately ceased to exist. These were in three old mills that stood along the river. The mills had been there, in those identical places, since the time of the Moors. But some months back they had been purchased by the Seville Electric Company. All the power in the river was to be used for electricity; there was no longer any left for the mills. "And so it goes," the tobacconist said, lapsing into Spanish. "We of Ronda did not want to see the mills sold and the mill-owners did not want to sell them, but that had no bearing on the matter. By one means and another, the millowners were forced out. I understand the papers in Seville reported that the millowners were paid good prices, but in truth they were destroyed."

It interested the tobacconist to learn that I was an American. Not many Americans came to Ronda, he said, but a long time ago there had been one, a rich gentleman named Rothschild, who lived in the town for many years. Was I perhaps acquainted with the descendants of this Señor Rothschild? I made an effort to explain that as a rule England, not the United States, was the home of wealthy Rothschilds, but I did not get far. The Señor Rothschild in question, I was assured, had indeed been an American, and a very, very rich one. There were some old people in Ronda—really ancient ones—who remembered how he used to walk down the street scattering money among the children as he passed. The ancient ones remembered this well, for they had been among the children. They spoke of Señor Rothschild with much affection. He had brought a string of riding horses to Ronda and had eventually gone insane. Nobody was surprised. The ancient ones said that even as children they had known it was coming sooner or later.

Something in the tobacconist's manner as he told me all this made me suspect that a sort of inverted syllogism had been worked out in the kitchens and wineshops of Ronda —Señor Rothschild was rich and crazy, Señor Rothschild was an American, therefore all Americans are rich and crazy—but I may have been wrong. And I must admit that even if I was right, the tobacconist did not act like a man who had accepted this line of reasoning. For just then my wife returned, and he introduced himself formally—Hernando Carril was his name—and said that if it would give us pleasure he would be glad to show us around the town at our convenience. Señora Carril, he assured us, could look

after his customers. We gladly accepted his offer and arranged to meet him in his shop at ten o'clock the next
morning.

It was nearly dark by the time we got back to our room.
A cold wind was blowing from the mountains. We tried
sitting on the balcony where we had had coffee, but now
it was too uncomfortable. And it was almost as cold in our
room as on the balcony. The dinner hour is late in Spain
—generally ten o'clock, at the earliest—and though our
hotel, like some others, opened its dining room at nine, we
still had an hour to go. We thought of finding a café where
we could have a drink and maybe get warm, and then
decided to do our drinking downstairs in the hotel. We
hadn't seen a café that looked as if it might be warm, and
it seemed simpler to stay where we were.

We wished, though, that the downstairs surroundings
were a bit more cheerful. Coming in from our walk, we
had noticed that most of the public rooms were dark and
that the few lights burning in the others barely shook off
the shadows. Still wondering about the history of the hotel,
I went into the hall bathroom to wash up, and there I
found a clue. All the fixtures had been manufactured in
England; "TWYFORDS-HENLEY," they were marked. "But of
course!" I said to myself. "This place was English-built."
That explained the way the garden was laid out and the
spacious attempt at comfort, and, when we went downstairs, it helped explain our fellow guests. There were eight
of them—five women and three men—and they were all

English. They acknowledged our presence, as the English sometimes do, by pretending that we were not there. While we were waiting in the library for our drinks, I heard one lady say to another that she lived in Sussex and that her father was a colonel who used to visit Ronda when he was stationed at Gibraltar. I glanced at some of the books on the shelves: big-game hunting in Africa; a doctor's life in India; a regimental history of the Queen's Rifles; "Helbeck of Bannisdale," by Mrs. Humphry Ward; George Meredith's "Beauchamp's Career." A copy of H. G. Wells' "The Outline of History" had a fiercely modern look.

But still there was something about the hotel that eluded me. I felt that I knew what I was after, and it irritated me not to be able to put my finger on it. I reminded myself to ask Señor Carril to tell me about the place. The building of such a hotel would have been no small event in Ronda, and the tobacconist, close as he was to the old people, would certainly know all the details.

I am afraid that when Señor Carril showed us the town the next morning, he found me a rather indifferent sightseer. Had it not been for my wife, he might even have regretted his friendly gesture. As I have already suggested, the truth is that, except for its view, Ronda does not have a great deal to offer: ancient defense walls; the Moorish section, just as it was when the Moors lived there; a crumbling mansion of many courtyards, built in 1042; an undistinguished cathedral; and, to me the most impressive of the lot, the oldest existing bull ring in Spain.

According to the people of Ronda, who do not allow their pride of place to lead them very far astray, the art of bullfighting, as practiced in Spain today, more or less began in their city. Developed in Spain by the Moors and then appropriated by the Spaniards, bullfighting was originally an aristocratic pastime; even Charles V had a crack at it. A four-foot lance was the only weapon used in those days, and the men fought from horseback. Toward the end of the seventeenth century, professionals took over the sport, and the first great one was a Rondeño named Francisco Romero. It was he who introduced both the *estoque* (the short sword for killing the bull) and the *muleta* (the small, heart-shaped red flag used by the bullfighter to execute his final passes and to control the bull at the kill). This was sometime around 1700, and Romero, by his accomplishment, notched himself a place in Spanish history just a few inches below the Cid. Where Romero immortalized himself is not known exactly. It couldn't have been in the Ronda ring, because that wasn't built until 1784. Erected by a company of gentlemen who had gathered themselves into an organization called the Real Maestranza de Cabelleria de Ronda, the ring was first used for displays and contests of horsemanship, and perhaps some bullfights in the old manner—with a lance and on horseback. Around 1800, the building became an out-and-out bull ring, and shortly thereafter Spain's first bullfighting school was opened in Ronda—an institution where young aspirants could learn their trade under the tutelage of scarred, experienced hands. "So here is the birthplace," Señor Carril said. "Here it began."

The bull ring struck me as being the handsomest building in Ronda—and, for that matter, with its combination of severe simplicity and expensive elegance, one of the most attractive small buildings in all Spain. It has a reddish-yellow tile roof and a white circular wall pierced by a number of small, barred windows that give so much of Spain its guarded, hidden look, and the entrance gate, flanked by two beige-colored marble columns, is adorned with an intricate wrought-iron balcony in the high-rococo style. The ring, built in two tiers, differs from all others in that it has a canopy, made of wood, over its seats. The circular procession of precisely spaced slender columns supporting the arches that, in turn, support the canopy gives Ronda's ring an intimacy and coziness that must make a bullfight there seem almost a family entertainment.

The Ronda ring seats ten thousand spectators. Once the largest ring in the country, it is now one of the smallest. Indeed, the arena proper is so small that Rondeños scornfully accuse the big-city bullfighters of being afraid to appear there because, with so little room for maneuvering, they run too great a risk of being gored. I could see that my friend Señor Carril felt strongly about the matter, and that only my wife's presence kept him from letting go completely. But it could be that the issue is more one of cash than of courage. On the basis of the fees that a ranking bullfighter can command in bigger arenas, Ronda must be placed in the category of a tank town. The bull ring is consequently used but once a year, on May 20, when every-body turns out for the start of a three-day feria commem-orating the Moors' surrender of Ronda to the Christians.

My interest in the bull ring had not caused me to lose interest in the hotel. When finally our tour was over and we were accompanying Señor Carril back to his shop, I asked him about it. He seemed surprised by my curiosity. Yes, he knew the history of the hotel. It was built in 1898 by an Englishman named McInton—a retired mining engineer who had settled in Gibraltar. There were many in Ronda who remembered him well. He was a tall man, with red-dish hair and blue eyes, who never really learned to speak Spanish. In this respect, he was not found as sympathetic as Señor Rothschild. Señor Rothschild spoke Spanish with grace and authority. The old people considered him just as well bred as they were.

"But the hotel," I said. "How did McInton come to build it?"

Señor Carril shrugged. "When he first came to Ronda, staying at an inn near the bull ring, nobody thought of him as a rich man," he said. "However, when he started building the hotel, pouring into it only God knows how many millions of pesetas, it began to be rumored that he was nearly as rich as Señor Rothschild. In his life as a min-ing engineer he may have found a gold mine. Who knows?"

It was easy to see that McInton was not remembered quite as affectionately in Ronda as Señor Rothschild. I asked a few more questions, but Señor Carril had run out of information. All he could tell me was that the hotel was believed to be having trouble making ends meet. There had been a time, he said, when many English people came to Ronda—especially the English who lived on Gibraltar— but lately fewer had been coming every year. It had something to do with their money, he added, though what this was he didn't know. He gave it as his opinion that if things continued as they were, the hotel would have to close its doors.

This I had already suspected. But what I was searching for was something else—something that I still could not quite define. We left Señor Carril at his shop, went to the hotel for lunch, and then took a walk in the country. Arriving back at the hotel around four o'clock, we found that our walk had made us hungry, so we ordered a small meal of bread, butter, jam, and coffee and ate it on the hotel's piazza, looking out across the garden at the view. There are hundreds of swallows in Ronda, making their homes in the cracks and crevices of the gorge, and some of them were flying about. A big green lizard—the biggest lizard I have ever seen—was sunning itself on one of the garden paths.

For a while there wasn't a sound. We watched the swallows and the lizard, and I don't think that I could have felt myself to be deeper in Spain. Then, from inside the hotel, someone searched out a few chords on a piano. They seemed actually to break through the silence, leaving a ripped, shattered place. After a pause the piano was struck more purposefully and a soprano voice began singing "On

the Road to Mandalay." The voice and the song hung on
the edge of absurdity for a moment—Oh no! Not here! Not
in this eagle's nest of a town high in the mountains of
Spain!—but then, when the singer, flatting just a little, got
to the tricky part where the dawn comes up like thunder
out of China across the bay, the voice and the song, instead of seeming absurd, were exactly in place and entirely
correct.

The elusive thing that I had been searching for finally
came to me, and I wondered how I could have been so
long in grasping it. For what this hotel was, as I needed
"On the Road to Mandalay" to make me realize (sung, it
pleased me to imagine, by the spinster daughter of an English colonel who had once been stationed at Gibraltar),
was one of the last reminders of the great days of European
travel—the period, extending up to 1900, or even a decade
later—when if one ventured into Spain it was still possible
to be rewarded with something of the same sense of per-
sonal discovery that such earlier travelers as Borrow and
Ford experienced. The world hadn't yet shrunk. It took a
certain amount of doing to get from England to the peninsula, and an even greater amount of doing to get to Ronda.
After such a trial, one wanted to settle down for a while.
One was grateful to Mr. McInton for making things almost as nice as they were at home. There were picnics,
walks in the hills, diaries to be written up, new novels like
"Helbeck of Bannisdale" to be read, the pleasure of the
post when it arrived, and simply the thrill of knowing (and
here I see a covey of dainty, chattering girls in fresh white

muslin dresses cut on princess lines, and wide straw hats with colored ribbons, pink and yellow and blue) that there were bandits and brigands in the hills—dark, lean, romantically handsome men with white teeth, who played guitars.

It was like that then, and there is no reason to believe that it will ever be like that again. Travel has become tourism and is ruled by the clock. There are buses that cover the whole Grand Tour in a little over a month. It's the tourist trade that Europe is now geared for, and even Spain is bound to succumb. In Torremolinos, a seaside resort near Málaga, I saw a roadside restaurant that was built to resemble a battleship: I thought it would look rather extreme in Hollywood, but since I was only getting back what we export, I couldn't very well quarrel with it. I am afraid, however, that it is part of a trend. Any number of new hotels have been built in Spain recently, a few so slick and shiny that they might have sprung full-chromed from the brain of Mr. Conrad Hilton himself, and many others are going up. The Costa Brava—that part of Spain's Mediterranean coastline that runs north from Barcelona to the French border—is having an out-and-out boom.

So it does not seem unlikely that Señor Carril and some other hardheaded citizens of Ronda with whom I spoke are right. Ronda is miles away from the tourist run—bad roads: no amusements to speak of—and who would want to go to all that trouble just to look at some mountains? I do not think that these people of Ronda are being unduly pessimistic. Should the present trend persist—and what is there to reverse it?—it appears almost inevitable that Mr.

McInton's hotel will have to close its doors. And what of Ronda then? Well, who knows? *Sabe Dios, señores y señoras, quién sabe?* I believe, however, that a few things may be predicted. They will tell in the kitchens and wine-shops how it used to be in the old days (though the ancient ones who remember when Mr. McInton built his hotel and how Señor Rothschild used to walk down the street scattering money as he passed will have long been dead by then), and the hotel will slowly go to pieces (the blinds sagging, the porch decaying, the empty rooms filled with gloom), and the swallows will fly above the lost, ruined garden, wheeling and diving against the unadmired view.

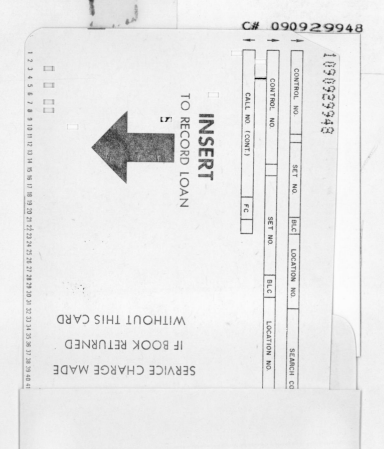

INSERT

TO RECORD LOAN

CONTROL NO. | SET NO. | BLC | LOCATION NO. | SEARCH CO

CONTROL NO. | SET NO. | BLC | LOCATION NO.

CALL NO. (CONT.) | FC

SERVICE CHARGE MADE
IF BOOK RETURNED
WITHOUT THIS CARD

1 2 3 4 5 6 7 8 9 10 11 12 13 14 15 16 17 18 19 20 21 22 23 24 25 26 27 28 29 30 31 32 33 34 35 36 37 38 39 40 41